YOUR TECHNOLOGY OUTREACH ADVENTURE

YOUR TECHNOLOGY OUTREACH ADVENTURE

Tools for Human-Centered Problem Solving

Erin Berman

ALA
Editions   CHICAGO | 2019

ERIN BERMAN is a librarian of international intrigue who, when not serving her community, enjoys late 1990s science fiction films, satirical art pieces, and friendly British baking championships.

»»»

© 2019 by the American Library Association

Extensive effort has gone into ensuring the reliability of the information in this book; however, the publisher makes no warranty, express or implied, with respect to the material contained herein.

ISBNs
978-0-8389-1778-7 (paper)
978-0-8389-1787-9 (PDF)
978-0-8389-1786-2 (ePub)
978-0-8389-1788-6 (Kindle)

Library of Congress Cataloging-in-Publication Data
Names: Berman, Erin, author.
Title: Your technology outreach adventure : tools for human-centered problem solving / Erin Berman.
Description: Chicago : ALA Editions, an imprint of the American Library Association, 2018. | Includes bibliographical references.
Identifiers: LCCN 2018024640| ISBN 9780838917787 (print : alk. paper) | ISBN 9780838917862 (epub) | ISBN 9780838917879 (pdf) | ISBN 9780838917886 (kindle)
Subjects: LCSH: Library outreach programs--United States. | Technological literacy—Study and teaching—Activity programs—United States. | Libraries—Information technology—United States. | Libraries and community—United States.
Classification: LCC Z711.7 .B47 2018 | DDC 027.4/2—dc23
LC record available at https://lccn.loc.gov/2018024640

Cover design by Krista Joy Johnson. Text design and composition by Karen Sheets de Gracia in the Freight Text, Museo, and Big Noodle typefaces.

♾ This paper meets the requirements of ANSI/NISO Z39.48–1992 (Permanence of Paper).

Printed in the United States of America
23 22 21 20 19   5 4 3 2 1

CONTENTS

PREFACE

W hat does it mean to be technology literate in today's world? It is more than just understanding how to perform a Google search for a new apple pie recipe. Technology-literate citizens of the world are able to adapt quickly to changes. They are critical thinkers who explore creative uses of technology devices. Those who are technology literate do not have an innate fear of new devices; they are comfortable with failure and confident in trying new things. Technology-literate people no longer view new technology as magic; they understand how things work and know how to find answers when they face stumbling blocks. All of these factors lead to a citizenry that is excited about learning new technology and finding ways of integrating it into their everyday lives.

The twenty-first century has ushered in an era of integrated technology lifestyles. We live in a world where 77 percent of Americans have a smartphone in their pockets and 95 percent have a cellphone of some kind.[1] We are connected to the global community in an unprecedented way. Technology now touches every part of our lives, whether we have embraced it or not. For many of us, our screens are the first thing we touch in the morning and the last thing we interact with before going to sleep. Technological devices are deeply embedded in our lives but are also in a constant state of flux. Every day a new update comes out, a new device is announced, and we all struggle to adapt to this quickly changing environment.

This rapid change creates excitement in many and anxiety in others. Technology has opened up a myriad of doors, unlocking access to nearly the entirety of human knowledge. Yet, it has also created barriers for those who are not in the know. Those who do not have the means or knowledge to keep up with the latest tech trends may find themselves quickly being left behind. Libraries have unlocked an opportunity to continue their work as the great equalizers of society by bringing technology literacy into their traditional programming repertoire.

Being technology literate is a critical part of successful living today. Many people experience a great deal of fear around technology, and this includes library staff. We are fearful of breaking something expensive, of embarrassing ourselves when what we're trying to do doesn't work, of being unable to teach others how to use the technology themselves. Such fears are compounded when we consider bringing technology outside the library's walls.

Although these are valid fears, they are ones we can overcome. Once we discover the technology needs of our communities, we can reframe how we approach teaching technology literacy. We begin by understanding that we are not teaching the technology itself. Instead, we are teaching critical thinking; technology is simply the tool we use to teach this process. Additionally, we are using the library's resources to give people exposure to technology they may not be able to afford at home. This brings people into the connected world; they can put their hands on something they heard about in the news instead of just seeing it as another stumbling block to overcome.

Many libraries across the country have seen the need to develop technology literacy programming in their buildings. Libraries are building makerspaces, teaching coding, and hosting e-reader trainings. The people who come into the library seeking access to technology are gaining it! Yet, with so much fear surrounding technology, many are reluctant to seek help. Some people may not even feel comfortable in the library and so are not likely to visit, much less consider coming in for a program on a topic they know nothing about or even see a need for in their day-to-day lives. In-library programs can reach only the people who choose to come into the library.

Such limited audiences and the common fears surrounding technology present a unique opportunity for libraries. Librarians can now mix traditional outreach models with the technology programming we are already perfecting. By blending these services we can reach people in the spaces where they feel comfortable, such as churches or laundromats, parks or senior centers. By adopting technology outreach as a standard practice, we remove barriers to access. People will be more comfortable working with unfamiliar technology tools when they are in familiar spaces, and when they have permission to fail.

I designed this book to give you the tools you need to create strong technology-based outreach programming. We'll begin with an exploration of outreach basics and the specific needs that come with adding technology to your outreach. Then, we'll look at human-centered design thinking through exercises that will teach you how to get to know your community and how to design outreach programs that keep people front and center. The tools that I present through these exercises will help to ease the technology fears your staff may feel, giving them a safe place to fail successfully. Last, we'll look at some real-world case studies of technology outreach programs from my work as Innovations Manager at the San José Public Library.

Reaching beyond the walls of our libraries is critical because our most at-need populations are often those who do not have access to our library buildings. This is especially true in rural locations or in areas with limited services. We have to meet people where they are. Libraries provide the platform that enables us to connect people to technology and to teach them critical thinking and creative problem solving. When we alleviate our fears about combining technology and outreach, doors will open to a whole new world of programming options. It is my hope that this book will help you to connect with your community in new ways, to approach solving problems with new tools, and to reach new populations through technology.

NOTE

1. "Mobile Fact Sheet," Pew Research Center, "Internet and Technology," February 5, 2018, www.pewinternet.org/fact-sheet/mobile.

ACKNOWLEDGMENTS

Working with technology means being flexible, adapting quickly to change, thinking critically, failing successfully, and, perhaps most important, seeking help whenever you need it. None of the feats we accomplish in life are done without the help of others. This book would not have been possible without the response to my own call for support from my incredible library colleagues.

A huge thank-you is extended to Megan Tristao, Amelia Vander Heide, and Julie Oborny for lending their critical eyes to the editing process. I also want to thank Sharon Fung who pulled me onto the design thinking train. Lastly, I am forever thankful to the amazingly supportive staff at San José Public Library for working with me on all of our technology-based outreach initiatives.

BRIDGING THE DIGITAL DIVIDE

For generations, librarians have been the gatekeepers to knowledge. They have preserved history in the tombs of texts, unlocking passages for those who entered through their doors. Information was not always immediately accessible in your pocket like it is today. Instead, if you wanted to tap into the knowledge of the world, you had to venture down to the local library, tiptoe your way through endless stacks of books, and spend hours getting lost in microfiche. The library held all of the information within its materials, and the librarians were there to instruct you on how to access it all. Their combined mission was to serve information needs—to teach literacy.

TRADITION IN LITERACY INSTRUCTION

Although walking into a modern-day library may feel very different from entering the charming rooms locked away in your memory, the library's mission remains the same: literacy. When we get to the core of what a public library is for, we always return to literacy. One of the library's roles in our society is to teach people the skills needed to be competent in a certain area, to possess knowledge. The library exists to create informed citizens who can be their best possible selves and also be engaged in the democracy of their communities. In today's world, libraries are looking at literacy through a new lens.

A librarian's job used to be primarily about reading literacy. Beginning with young children, a librarian's work revolved around teaching people how to unlock the information held within the texts that lined the library walls. The librarian taught search strategies, how to evaluate sources, and critical-thinking skills. Without the Internet, there were limited pathways to accessing knowledge. The library was the place you would go to gain the skills and knowledge needed to interact with the world around you. Today's librarians still do all these things, but they now have additional literacies to teach.

With the advent of the Internet and the explosion of technology, people began finding their information in new ways; they explored and interacted with the world differently from how they had in the past. Large segments of the population are now connected to the Internet in some fashion (e.g., via broadband or mobile phone service). According to the Pew Research Center, "Adoption rates are only one component of the digital divide, however. A person's comfort level with technology and the rate in which they use the internet at work and in their everyday lives also varies by income group."[1] Even as more people become connected, those at lower socioeconomic levels still struggle with adoption.

Libraries, being the great equalizer, jumped at the opportunity to level the playing field in the quest for knowledge and were some of the first places to offer the public free access to computers and later the Internet. With these new technological tools, librarians found themselves needing to teach people how to unlock the knowledge trapped behind a screen.

ACCESS AND KNOWLEDGE

Libraries may be the only place where some people are able to access technology. However, equality of access cannot happen if people are unfamiliar with how the technology works in the first place. Our responsibility as librarians is to put together programming and resources that assist people in learning these technologies. We have to go beyond just basic computer classes and simply teaching patrons how to use a device. Instead, we are charged with assisting people in becoming critical thinkers so they can adapt quickly when technology changes. Today's world is complicated, and navigating through it can be frustrating and overwhelming for many. Some will become overwhelmed by their frustration, choosing not to adapt at all and setting themselves up to be left behind.

With an ever-changing technology landscape, what can we do to ensure no one in our society is left behind? How can we ensure that those people in our communities who are afraid of adopting technology, or who don't have access to it, can gain the skills needed to participate fully as twenty-first-century citizens? Although we may have the latest and greatest technology residing within the walls of our libraries, it can serve only those who walk through our doors.

In 2016, the Pew Research Center found that 29 percent of the lowest adopters of technology, those living in households making $30,000 or less a year, have never visited a library; yet, 80 percent of respondents said they felt the library had great value and should offer programs to teach people digital skills.[2] The great news is that many libraries across the United States already do this, from computer classes to coding workshops. Still, with nearly all these offerings happening within the physical library space, those 29 percent of low technology adopters who do not visit the library are being left behind. Even the majority of library visitors are not participating in technology-based programming; only 27 percent of patrons attended a library program in 2016.[3] We need to discover a new way of providing access to technology and technology training in order to reach all our citizens who are in need.

FEAR OF TECHNOLOGY

One of the primary reasons people avoid technology is fear. This fear keeps many people from even connecting to the Internet and becomes stronger in the face of emerging high-tech tools. Such strong feelings of apprehension based on a perceived threat may cause people to feel too embarrassed to come into a library to ask for help.

Although it may be easy for most of us to think of a library as a safe and welcoming place, the library can be intimidating for those who do not understand how it works or what it has to offer. On top of that, there is a psychological cost to asking for help. People may feel uncomfortable seeking help, either because they think they might be bothering someone or because they are afraid of being seen as incompetent.[4] Lots of people experience fear surrounding technology—fear of the unknown, of failing, of looking like a fool. Such fears are compounded when people are faced with learning something new in an unfamiliar, public space.

In 2015, Chapman University released its Survey of American Fears. The top three fears concerned technology. Christopher Bader, a professor of sociology at the university, explains:

> People tend to express the highest level of fear for things they're dependent on but that they don't have any control over, and that's almost the perfect definition of technology. You can no longer make it in society without using technology you don't understand to buy things at a store, to talk to other people, to conduct business. People are increasingly dependent, but they don't have any idea how these things actually work.[5]

If people need to interact with technology in order to navigate in this world but are too fearful to adopt the technology or learn how to use it, then we are faced with a major inequality within our society. Many technologies, and primarily the Internet, are our main sources for information gathering. We have to ensure that all of our residents know how to safely and confidently navigate through the high-tech world we are living in. One way we can do this is to go into the streets, meeting people where they already feel comfortable gathering.

BRINGING TECHNOLOGY INTO THE STREETS

Outreach is nothing new to libraries. Public libraries have acted as bridges out into communities for nearly as long as they have been active. In 1905, Mary Titcomb became the first to introduce the bookmobile to her community in the United States.[6] Titcomb identified a need for access to books in the remote rural areas of Washington County, Maryland. She was awarded a Carnegie grant of $2,500 that she used to create the nation's first outreach service. Since then, librarians all around the world have been seeking new ways to go beyond the walls of their libraries to serve people directly in the community.

Traditionally, library outreach has taken a few different forms, with the main purpose being to promote library services, not to deliver those services directly. Many of you will be familiar with this standard awareness-based type of outreach: Your library sends a librarian, you, to a community event or meeting to man a table that is stocked with leaflets and fliers about services and events back at the library. This style of outreach is all about marketing. Your job is to raise awareness about what the library is doing within its walls or through its website. Sometimes a small activity may also take place at the booth as a means to lure people in for a longer discussion about what the library has to offer.

Many libraries are taking this style of outreach one step further by setting up laptops and Wi-Fi hot spots in order to sign up people for library cards. This transforms an awareness-based outreach model into a service-based outreach model. These are some of the other common outreach programs that fall into this category:

> Storytimes
> Library instruction
> Bookmobiles
> Homebound delivery

One of the newest types of service-based outreach uses technology. Traditional bookmobiles are being converted into computer labs or technology filled buses. Librarians are teaching patrons how to use e-readers and check out e-books in addition to the standard library database instruction. This movement into technology-based outreach is what we'll be covering in this book. It can be the most intimidating type of outreach, but also the most rewarding.

Leaving the library to do outreach always presents a whole new set of challenges. Adding technology brings in an extra level of complexity. You might not even know where to begin beyond knowing that you want to offer some sort of technology-based outreach. That's okay! We'll begin in the next chapter by learning about the fundamentals that you will need to create successful technology-based outreach programs.

NOTES

1. Monica Anderson, "Digital Divide Persists Even as Lower-Income Americans Make Gains in Tech Adoption," Pew Research Center, "Fact Tank," March 22, 2017,

www.pewresearch.org/fact-tank/2017/03/22/digital-divide-persists-even-as-lower-income-americans-make-gains-in-tech-adoption.

2. John B. Horrigan, "Libraries 2016," Pew Research Center, "Internet and Technology," September 9, 2016, www.pewinternet.org/2016/09/09/libraries-2016.

3. Ibid., under "2. Library Usage and Engagement."

4. Bella M. Depaulo and Jeffrey D. Fisher, "The Costs of Asking for Help," *Basic and Applied Social Psychology* 1 (March 1980): 23–35.

5. Cited in Cari Romm, "Americans Are More Afraid of Robots Than Death," *The Atlantic*, October 16, 2015, www.theatlantic.com/technology/archive/2015/10/americans-are-more-afraid-of-robots-than-death/410929.

6. Nancy Smiler Levison, "Takin' It to the Streets: The History of the Book Wagon," *Library Journal* 116 (May 1991): 43–45.

OUTREACH FUNDAMENTALS

Technology-based outreach gives us the opportunity to offer a new set of programs to parts of our communities that may have very little interaction with the library. We can bring the high-level technology programming we are already offering within the walls of the library to new populations, meeting them in familiar areas where they are the most comfortable. Think of the library as a platform, not just a place. The services we offer through the library are meant to foster equality in society, giving every person equal opportunities to develop into their best possible selves. In our increasingly technology-centered world, the library is often the only place where some members of a community can gain access to technology training. We need to recognize, however, that many people face barriers to accessing technology programming within the library. This is why outreach is so vital.

Discovery and learning don't just happen within the walls of the library; they happen wherever users happen to be.[1] Although many libraries are adding makerspaces and technology labs to their physical buildings, not every library has the ability to add these new zones. A lack of money or space may prevent some libraries from building places where people can explore the digital world. These spaces also may not prove sufficient to serve library users at the bottom of the socioeconomic ladder, those who are the least likely to be able to take advantage of this digital learning in their everyday lives. Transportation to the library, limited library hours, apprehension surrounding using the library resources, lack of knowledge about what is happening in the library, or fear of technology are all common barriers to creating a technology-literate community.

For librarians, leaving the safety of our libraries to teach technology in our neighborhoods can initially feel intimidating. Our anxieties can be soothed by starting with a solid foundation of outreach best practices. Any technology-based outreach will follow the same basic principles of a standard outreach program. Getting a firm grasp on these best practices will ensure outreach success even with the addition of the technology components.

ALIGNING OUTREACH PROGRAMS WITH YOUR LIBRARY'S MISSION

Why does a library choose to do outreach? Most of us can look to our libraries' mission statements and strategic plans for guidance on why it is important for us to reach out to our communities. The San José Public Library mission states that the library "enriches lives by fostering lifelong learning and by ensuring that every member of the community has access to a vast array of ideas and information."[2] Enhancing access to every member of the community is a key component of the library's strategic priorities as well. As librarians, we cannot accomplish this without leaving the library to perform various outreach programs. Pull up your library's mission and strategic priorities. Which parts of them inform your outreach practice? Once you understand why your library has outreach services, you can move on to creating a plan and strategy for continued success.

UNDERSTANDING YOUR COMMUNITY

Through planning librarians can look at the bigger picture, examining "the needs of the community we serve and how we will respond to those needs, and determine what resources we need to accomplish our goals."[3] Our first step in this plan is to do a neighborhood assessment; figure 2.1 provides an example. We can use a variety of tools to determine the demographics of the neighborhoods our branches serve and, more important for outreach, whom we are not currently serving. Our assessments need to take a look at

PEARL AVENUE BRANCH PROFILE 2017

Service Area/Neighborhood Profile

Demographics

	#	%
Total population	42,464	100
Age breakdown		
Juvenile	8,493	20
Young Adult	1,274	3
Adult	28,026	66
Senior	4,671	11

Statistical Atlas in 95136: http://statisticalatlas.com/zip/95136/Overview

Analysis of effect: The Pearl Avenue Library is located in the Pinehurst neighborhood of San José. The total population of the Pinehurst neighborhood has decreased since 2011 by about 16 percent due to the increase of the cost of living in the area. Real estate prices are skyrocketing in all areas of the Bay Area and are pricing out low- to middle-class residents. The percentages per age range are still similar to the 2011 numbers, however.

Three Most Common Non-English Languages Spoken at Home and Percentage

- Spanish—15.9%
- Vietnamese—8.5%
- Tagalog—3.7%

Analysis of effect: The percentages of Spanish and Vietnamese speakers appear to be similar to the numbers provided in 2011. However, the number of Tagalog speakers at home seems to have exceeded the number of Chinese speakers in the neighborhood. This should alter the dynamics of the language collection, as Tagalog should now become a more targeted language at Pearl Avenue Library.

FIGURE 2.1 **Sample Neighborhood Assessment**

FIGURE 2.1 (continued)

School Enrollment

	#	%
Total persons 3+ years old	10,560	100.0
Total not enrolled	213	2.0
Total enrolled	10,347	98.0
In pre–primary school	921	8.9
In elementary or high school	6,187	59.8
In college	3,239	31.3

Analysis of effect: Twenty-four percent of the Pinehurst neighborhood is enrolled in school. As in 2011, a striking number of students are enrolled in college. Many students utilize the library's quiet room and request college-level material from San José State University. Because the borrowing process for Cal State items has changed, collegians in the Pinehurst neighborhood should be notified that they can still borrow San José State University items with their library cards using the interlibrary loan service. In addition, students still have access to the library's large database of scholarly journals.

Number of Schools Located within Walking Distance

- Elementary: 5 (Terrell Elementary/Carson Elementary/ Holy Family/Canoas Elementary/Parkview Elementary)
- Middle: 2 (John Muir Middle, Holy Family)
- High: 2 (Gunderson High, Broadway High)
- Special Day Classes (Erickson)
- University: 0
- Adult Education: 1 (Hillsdale Metro Ed Campus)

Major Community Features

Pearl Avenue Library is located at 4270 Pearl Avenue.

- Parks: Terrell, Vista, Thousand Oaks, and Waterford
- Community centers: Camden, Willow Glen, and Seven Trees
- Retail centers: Westfield Oakridge Mall, Capitol Expressway Auto Mall, and Almaden Plaza
- Churches: Holy Family, Calvary Chapel of San José, Hillsdale Evangelical Free, Cathedral of Faith
- Transportation: Easy access to Highways 87 and 85, the Capitol and Branham Light Rail Stations, Almaden Expressway, and Bus Line 70

FIGURE 2.1 (continued)

Analysis of effect: Pearl Avenue Library is located in a residential area close to Terrell Elementary and very near John Muir Middle. The Pinehurst neighborhood is densely populated and has a number of schools, businesses, and community services in the area.

Type of Community
(i.e., residential, business, industrial, age of homes)

The community is primarily residential with retail and commercial businesses concentrated on the surrounding major thoroughfares. According to the 2010 Census, 60 percent of homes are owned and 40 percent are rented. The majority of homes were built in the 1960s–1980s. A second construction surge occurred post-2000 in the area north of Capitol Expressway, bounded by Almaden Expressway and Monterey Highway.

Analysis of effect: The community is well established. Recent construction on the remaining large parcels of land in the area is high density. The timely expansion of Pearl Avenue Branch in 2008 coincided with the increased demand for library services that occurred in the post-2000 residential housing boom in the area.

Existing Partnerships

- Terrell Elementary YMCA Afterschool
- Carson Elementary R.O.C.K. Afterschool
- Erickson School
- Holy Family School
- Erickson Neighborhood Association
- Pinehurst Residents Association
- Redeemed Christian Church
- Central Valley Youth Soccer
- Girl Scouts of America
- Westbury Owners Association
- Alpha Kappa Alpha Society
- Santa Teresa Little League
- Robertsville Townhomes Homeowners Association
- Pinehurst Cabana Club
- Snell State Head Start
- Delia's Little Angel's Day Care
- Parkview Child Development Centers
- Terrell Elementary Special Day Classes

Report prepared by Ila Langner; final editing by Oscar Hernandez, Lucia Farnham-Hudson, Helen Kahn, and Erik Berman.

the whole community, not just the people who come into the library or those with whom the library regularly partners. A good neighborhood assessment paints an overall picture of a library's service area, helping us to discover the areas where we should focus our services and, in particular, our technology-based outreach.

Think of a neighborhood assessment as an opportunity to connect with the community you serve. Do not just sit at your computer and search the Internet for data. Go out into the neighborhood and speak with the local Chamber of Commerce, social services agencies, and advocacy groups to find out where people are gathering and what their needs are. Write down the local services and housing options that are available to the people living near your library; examples include day-care providers, schools, assisted-living facilities, parks, apartment complexes, and low-income housing facilities. All of these places are potential hot spots for engaging people through your future outreach programs.

Creating your library's neighborhood assessment enables you to quickly identify the needs of the community, helping you to choose appropriate locations for outreach. However, there is more to a neighborhood assessment than just a list of locations and demographics. You also need to speak directly to community members about what their needs are. We'll look at one method for doing this, the Hardwood Institute's guidelines for Turning Outward, in the next section.

HAVING MEANINGFUL COMMUNITY CONVERSATIONS

Turning Outward is when we take the steps needed to better understand our communities by "changing our processes and thinking to make our conversations more community-focused; being proactive to community issues; and putting community aspirations first."[4] The Harwood Institute for Public Innovation has partnered with the American Library Association to provide a fantastic set of tools to help librarians talk with their communities about aspirations and then develop programming to meet those goals and needs. Using the tools from the Harwood Institute can help your library in creating a more robust neighborhood assessment and in taking the first steps toward putting library patrons front and center in your design process.

There are many demographic tools available for gathering neighborhood data. Try these to get started:

> › American FactFinder (https://factfinder.census.gov)
> › Data.gov (www.data.gov)
> › StatisticalAtlas.com (https://statisticalatlas.com)
> › United States Census Bureau (www.census.gov)
> › Your city and/or county health department website
> › Your city, county, and/or local government website

Speaking with the community is a critical piece of understanding where your outreach services can do the most good. Later, in the How Do You Gain Insights from Stakeholders? section of chapter 6, you will learn additional methods for speaking with and observing your community. The conversations you have may be broad in scope, discussing overarching community needs, or focus more specifically on the problem your library is trying to solve through outreach programming. After intentional communication with your community, you will have a better understanding of what audiences might be best served through your outreach.

FINDING PARTNERS

Now that you have completed a neighborhood assessment, you can build a list of possible outreach sites. Narrow down this list by choosing locations where people regularly gather; piggybacking off an event that is already occurring at a location means a built-in audience. Consider adding your outreach program to the end of a preschool class or a senior lunch program. Attend local street fairs or a city council–sponsored neighborhood event.

Choosing a location that comes with an audience means less marketing work for your library. The people you are trying to help through your outreach program are those who are not already plugged into the regular library communication network. Meeting people in a comfortable place during an activity they are already familiar with will help ease them into accessing library services. This is especially important when your outreach involves technology, which may elicit feelings of anxiety for some people.

A **neighborhood assessment** should include the following information:

> › Demographics of the population the library serves
> › List of local services (e.g., parks, churches, community centers, preschools)
> › Community aspirations and needs
> › Library statistics or resources that your library offers to the public

Another added benefit to working at an outreach site that already offers programming is an opportunity to create new community partnerships. Talk with the owners of the site where you are looking to set up. Be clear about the resources you will need to make the outreach successful. Come prepared to partnership meetings with a list of questions that will help you to determine if the partnership will work for both organizations. I often use a questionnaire (see figure 2.2) during the initial meeting with a potential partner to ensure that the relationship will meet their needs as well as ours. It's important to avoid jumping into relationships simply because they are offered, without considering whether they will work for your library and your patrons. Your library has a lot to offer in a partnership. Prepare a list of questions that will assist you in sharing what you bring to the table and in understanding what the potential partner can offer. After the initial interview, you will have a reference sheet to use in evaluating whether the partnership will meet all your needs.

>>

Outreach can be successful only when you understand the needs and aspirations of your community, including those you do not currently serve. You have to be intentional, aligning your outreach programming strategy with the library's mission. An in-depth analysis of your community and library will enable you to take the next step in creating a formal outreach plan.

PARTNER NAME: _____

Setting Clear Expectations

- What are our expectations for this partnership?
- What can we offer?
- What can they offer?

Funding

- Do you need funding from us to make the program run?
  If so, how much?
- Are there funds available to support this program through grants
  or other options?

Learning Objectives and Measurable Outcomes

- How will you measure and identify learning objectives
  and outcomes?

Staffing Needs

- Do you need our staff to assist during the program?
  If so, how many and to what extent?
- Do you need our staff to assist in program development?

Time

- How often would you like the program to run?
  Once, twice, ongoing?
- What is the program length?
- Would the program run concurrently (multiple sessions in one day)?

Location

- What is the ideal location for the program?
- Will any other locations work? (If you already have locations in mind,
  give those as options to see if there is interest.)

Audience

- Is there a particular demographic in mind?

FIGURE 2.2 **Partnership Questionnaire**

NOTES

1. John G. Palfrey, *Bibliotech: Why Libraries Matter More Than Ever in the Age of Google* (New York: Basic Civitas Books, 2013).

2. "Mission and Vision," San José Public Library, accessed June 13, 2018, www.sjpl.org/mission.

3. Jeannie Dilger-Hill and Erica MacCreaigh, *On the Road with Outreach: Mobile Library Services* (Santa Barbara, CA: Libraries Unlimited, 2010), 3.

4. "Turning Outward Resources for Libraries," American Library Association, "Tools, Publications and Resources," accessed June 13, 2018, www.ala.org/tools/librariestransform/libraries-transforming-communities/resources-for-library-professionals.

TECHNOLOGY-BASED OUTREACH PLANNING

S ome outreach programming can be thrown together without much planning. Your library may even keep an outreach supply kit on hand for those last-minute opportunities at community events or schools. Staff can quickly go out and disseminate information about library services, setting up a table to hand out fliers, bookmarks, and event calendars. Technology-based outreach takes more planning to ensure success.

After you have determined why your library wants to do outreach and the needs of the community, you will have to build an outreach plan. Structuring a plan includes choosing potential sites, purchasing your technology, finding the funds to pay for the outreach, and confronting your fear of failure. Addressing all of these aspects of your program, before even determining the outreach details, can help you move confidently through the design process and into implementation.

CHOOSING OUTREACH SITES

You have performed a neighborhood assessment that assisted you in creating a list of potential partners for outreach programs and spaces in which to host them. How do you break that list down into spaces that would be the most successful for technology-based outreach? You need to consider a new set of conditions that may not regularly be on your radar when choosing a location for a standard outreach program. When determining a technology-based outreach location, keep the following in mind:

> **Access to power.** Are there easily accessible power outlets? Will they be available during the outreach program or will they be in use by someone else? Sometimes you may see a power outlet during the initial site tour only to discover on the day you show up that it is inside a locked building or being used for another program. Do you need an extension cord? Will cords be provided or do you need to bring your own? How long do they need to be? If there is no power available, can you provide your own generator? Generators can be extremely helpful but also are noisy, require gas, and cannot be used inside. Can you use devices that do not require power from an electrical outlet?

> **Wireless Internet.** Do you need to have access to the Internet in order to run your program? How reliable is the Wi-Fi at the site? Will the Wi-Fi work if there are multiple people on the network at the same time? Does your technology work only if there is Internet access? Some tools require a network connection in order to operate. Look into this when you are selecting which technology to use. Can you purchase mobile hot spots to supplement site-provided Wi-Fi?

> **Physical space.** Does your program require people to sit or can they work comfortably while standing? Is there enough space to work with a large group all at once or will you be doing one-on-one training? If you will be working with small groups or one-on-one, how will people sign up? Will you need to provide your own furniture? Make sure that the furniture you want to use can fit inside your outreach vehicle and is easy for staff to set up.

> **Program length.** It can take a long time to teach someone how to be comfortable with technology. Oftentimes an outreach program is short, allowing for only a passing interaction with each person. The outreach location you choose will have a huge impact on the type of program

you create. If the plan is to do outreach as part of a larger community event, you might consider doing a show-and-tell or drop-in style of program. This type of outreach program gives people the opportunity to touch and interact with the technology but is not designed to turn them into experts. With this style of outreach, interaction is limited but serves to create excitement and intrigue; use it to promote further learning opportunities available at the library. More detailed training programs require a different setup. You will want to make sure that you can interact with a small group or one-on-one with people in a space that supports limited interruptions. This outreach style will enable you to teach more advanced technology literacy skills.

› **Repeatability.** Can you visit the same site on multiple occasions, and is it possible to secure the same audience for these different visits? Increasing a person's comfort level with technology often requires multiple interactions with that person. Doing a series of outreach programs with the same audience can be a great way to improve people's skill sets. This can be extremely challenging, so don't let it get you down if you are unable to secure this type of setup. Often a site will want you to visit multiple times, but it can be nearly

Try some of these technology-based outreach ideas:

› Library card sign-up
› Laptops and mobile hot spot lending at the laundromat
› Computer workshops for new immigrants at a Social Security office
› E-book training for the homebound
› Learning to code sessions with the whole family at back-to-school night
› Getting up-to-date with technology classes for incarcerated adults
› Creating laser-cut photo puzzles at the senior center
› Providing non-Internet-accessible e-readers and training at prisons
› Making brooches with LEDs (light-emitting diodes) at an after-school program
› Building robots at a community fair

impossible to interact with the same set of people at each event. Determine if your outreach program will be a one-time class or a series of classes with each building upon the learning from the previous session.

> **Environment.** The environment for your technology outreach is an important consideration in terms of comfort, practicality, and safety. What will the temperature be? Will people be comfortable interacting with technology while standing in the hot sun? Will the technology work in a rainy environment? Where is the sun going to be located during the event? If you are using laptops, you may find that the screens are not visible in direct sunlight. Is there parking for your mobile outreach vehicle? Does the site meet ADA (Americans with Disabilities Act) accessibility requirements once you have set up? If you are providing homebound services, what measures have you put in place to ensure staff safety?

PURCHASING TECHNOLOGY

You also need to consider the type of technology you are planning to bring to your outreach. First, assess if your community needs access to that particular technology. Look back at your neighborhood assessment. Does the technology you are looking at using meet your community's needs and aspirations?

Try some of these technology tools in your outreach programming:

> E-readers
> Tablets
> Laptops
> Video cameras
> DSLR (digital single-lens reflex) cameras
> Smartphones
> Makey Makey

> Arduino
> 3-D printers
> Vinyl cutters
> Sewing machines
> Paper circuits
> Cardboard VR (virtual reality)
> Robotics (LEGO MINDSTORMS/BOOST, Sphero, UBTECH Jimu, Cleverbot)

Far too often librarians will choose technology based on "technolust" rather than an identified need. Expensive technology devices may quickly find themselves gathering dust on a librarian's desk rather than serving the community. Choose technology that meets community needs and then evaluate your outreach based on how well that technology is meeting those needs.[1]

The information you have discovered by speaking with the people in your neighborhood will help guide you in evaluating what types of technology will fit the needs of your community. More detailed surveys and interviews with the intended audience for the outreach can also be illuminating. Guidance on how to perform these conversations can be found in the How Do You Gain Insights from Stakeholders section of chapter 6. Create a short list of tools that could be used at the potential sites you have chosen. A technology device may be well suited for one environment but fail in another. Something that may work perfectly in the fairly stable environment of a school may not perform well in a park or on a mobile bus.

Consider the level of training it takes to be proficient on a piece of technology. If the outreach is about creating excitement and involves limited interaction time, you might want to pick a flashy piece of new technology that people aren't likely to have in their homes. If the goal is to teach basic skills, then choose technology that is commonplace and practical. Also, take into consideration the level of training that staff will need to become competent enough themselves to instruct others; give staff plenty of time to play with the new technology before leaving the library. It is likely they will have to do troubleshooting on site; the more familiar they are with the technology, the less frustrating this will be.

There are many exciting technology tools for your library to choose from to use as part of an outreach program. When you are ready to purchase something, look for a retailer that will let you test the tool first, and consider the following when you interact with the technology for the first time:

> How robust is it? Can it withstand traveling? Is it waterproof? Does it need a case to prevent damage from falls?

> How easy is it to use? Did you struggle to figure out how to turn it on or was it user friendly?

> Are there accessibility issues? Will all patrons be able to use the device? Are there special tools or software you need to make it accessible?

> Can you add security locks or other antitheft mechanisms? Is there a place to put library cataloging stickers?

PAYING FOR THE OUTREACH PROGRAM

A common misconception is that technology programming has to be expensive. Although many technology tools out there cost a great deal of money (e.g., 3-D printers, laser cutters, virtual reality rigs), you are likely to find that the tools with the most impact on a user's daily life are the least expensive. Do not be intimidated by the high price of emerging technology. Your library can start by exploring low-cost options such as paper circuits instead of diving straight into laser cutters.

Unless you are planning on building a mobile technology lab, it is a good idea to start out with less-expensive, easy-to-use technology when you begin experimenting with this new style of outreach. Starting small and inexpensive will also help when pitching your idea to library management. You always run the risk of tools being broken when you bring technology into the streets. This cost of doing business should be factored into the scope of the project, not used as a barrier to doing anything at all.

Consider seeking funding through library friends groups and grants. Since you have already spent time speaking with the community, approach local businesses to ask for support. The knowledge gained during your neighborhood assessment can be used to tell the story of why this outreach will be important for the community. Later in this book, you will learn about tools that can assist you when speaking to stakeholders about the impact of your outreach. You will also discover how to evaluate your program so that you can pitch it successfully and show a return on investment to the stakeholders who supported your outreach. Remember, it never hurts to ask for funding for a program. The worst that can happen is that you are told no, which is the same answer you started with before asking.

FACING YOUR FEAR OF FAILURE

Failure is always an option when we are pushing our boundaries and trying new things, like technology-based outreach! The key is to learn how to fail successfully. Many people are scared of technology because they are afraid of breaking something. However, those who are the most adept at using technology are constantly pushing buttons and trying new things. They set aside the fear of something going wrong. Instead of fearing failure, we have to learn how to troubleshoot and iterate. We have to embrace that things are going to fail from time to time so that when they do, we can evaluate and learn from that failure.

Become comfortable with the fact that eventually the technology you are trying to teach will fail in the middle of your outreach program. It is unlikely that your IT (information technology) department will always be available to help out on-site. Give staff time to troubleshoot common problems at the branch before the first outreach event. Write up a troubleshooting guide and send it along as part of the outreach setup materials. Troubleshooting guides are the go-to resource for staff to check quickly for tested and tried solutions rather than trying to find help via Google in the middle of an outreach program. Documenting failures and solutions empowers staff to become problem solvers, building a collective knowledge database that will increase the future success of your outreach endeavors.

Learning how to fail successfully is an integral part of human-centered design thinking. Design thinking is a set of tools you can use to create your technology-based outreach programs. In the next section of this book, you'll learn how to take those neighborhood assessments and your lists of outreach locations and possible technology tools and turn them into successful technology-based outreach programs.

NOTE

1. John J. Burke, *The Neal-Schuman Library Technology Companion: A Basic Guide for Library Staff*, 4th ed. (Chicago: ALA Neal-Schuman, 2013).

4

DESIGN THINKING

Think about how most of us solve problems in the library. We may sit alone in our offices or gather with a group of our colleagues to decide what problem we are trying to solve. Often, one person will have already devised a solution to the problem; the group is really just convening to figure out how to implement the solution, not to evaluate the problem. There is often little room for creativity in these meetings. Staff are seldom given opportunities to explore multiple solutions quickly and cheaply. With the stakes so high, there is little room for failure. Instead, we are expected to succeed on the first pass.

The solution we create is rarely influenced by speaking with the population that will be served but rather by working from our own personal assumptions. If we hear only expert opinions or listen only to those who come into the library, we are working in an echo chamber that does not invite outside opinions. Decisions are based primarily on resources we currently have available instead of on community-based insights.

This traditional approach has driven libraries to create many amazing programs, but such an approach can impede forward progress in innovative service models. This is especially true when we begin to delve into areas our libraries have never explored. We need to shift our internal focus to one that embraces a human-centered design thinking approach. Design thinking gives us a way to look at and solve problems that keeps the people we are serving front and center at all times. Design thinking provides a framework for us to explore creatively while maintaining the public trust and being fiscally conservative.

HISTORY OF DESIGN THINKING

Design thinking or human-centered design began growing its roots in the mid-1950s. Born out of the engineering and scientific world, it was labeled "Comprehensive Anticipatory Design Science." Spearheaded by inventor Buckminster Fuller, design science used a systematic approach to problem solving; it considered design with the scientific method in mind. This allowed design to be based on "quantifiable facts, things that could be proven, measured, and improved on."[1]

Design science laid out the principles that became the foundation for much of design thinking today. It took a whole systems approach, looking at the project as a whole and anticipating impact. Michael Ben-Eli, founder of the Sustainability Laboratory, explains that design science encouraged "an active, open minded process of exploration and admission of error," which was necessary for the creative design process. It modeled itself on the scientific method, giving a set path to follow and space for iteration and evaluation along the way.[2] Although Fuller's process was iterative, using prototypes and embracing failures, it was not wholly user focused. Teams using the design science framework were composed primarily of experts within the field for which they were designing and did not directly involve the end user in the design process.

As Fuller continued developing the design science process, another similar approach to design was being formulated in Scandinavia. Coined "cooperative design" or "participatory design," this new approach began with Kristen Nygaard and his 1972 Norwegian Iron and Metal Workers Union project. Through this project, the world saw a shift "from traditional research and development of computer systems to working with people, directly changing and making more active the role of the local unions."[3] Nygaard's work inspired others throughout Scandinavia, beginning in Denmark, Sweden, and Norway with several other projects that focused on giving a voice to the end user.

The Scandinavian approach was built based on people's personal experiences. Design teams no longer operated in a vacuum, making all the decisions about how the product or service was going to behave. All stakeholders and potential stakeholders were brought in at the beginning of the design process. Building off Nygaard's work with the Norwegian Iron and Metal Workers Union, a new team began work in the early 1980s on the Utopia project, which was developed to "'give the end users a voice' in design and development of computer support in workplaces, thus enhancing the quality of the resulting system."[4] To achieve this, the Utopia project's team implemented the use of low-resolution prototypes (mock-ups of computer stations, organizational cards, etc.), early design sessions with users, and pilot implementation throughout the design process. Designers were now able to work directly with users throughout the process, iterating and improving designs based directly on user feedback.

Blossoming out of the work of Fuller and the Scandinavian design teams came IDEO and the fundamentals of what we today call human-centered design or design thinking. IDEO, formed in 1991 through a merger of three design companies owned by David Kelley, Bill Moggridge, and Mike Nuttall, spearheaded this new design movement. The company, now known as one of the leading design firms in the world, has used design thinking to innovate for such companies as Nike, Apple, and Bank of America. Building off the work that came before them, IDEO developed sets of tools and processes that could be used by anyone. Design is no longer limited to only designers. By using a framework for creative problem solving, anyone at any organization can design a solution to any given problem.

THE DESIGN THINKING MIND-SET

Libraries have recently begun adopting a new way of approaching and solving problems that puts them in tune with the needs of the public and opens an avenue to being nimble. This approach is called human-centered design or design thinking. Human-centered design is a way of thinking with tools for doing. There is no right or wrong path to creatively solving problems. When you begin to reframe your thought process as a human-centered one, you will be able to develop programs that solve real problems and not get swept away by the siren call of technolust. Thus, technology programs in particular benefit from planning through design thinking. The tools we learn can give us a road map to follow, but in the end, design thinking helps us to put people first, to design with people in mind, and to gain an understanding of why we are doing what we are doing.

Finding the why is critical to creating a successful technology-based outreach program. We shouldn't purchase technology and then just throw it out to the public without having a rationale for its use and an understanding of what its impact is supposed to be. How will we know if the program we are running is actually making a difference? What learning outcomes do we want participants to experience? If we do not know what the outcomes are supposed to be, and if we don't know why we are showcasing a piece of technology, then how will we measure the program's success?

Libraries are educational institutions, not just community recreation facilities. This means that librarians need to be working with a set of educational standards and best practices. Although we may not all be experts in pedagogy, we can use design thinking tools to help us develop quality outcomes-based programming. The design thinking process helps us to put intentionality into our endeavors and gives us the tools we need to evaluate our efforts. We can begin to tell stories about what we are doing, how it is working, and the lives that we are impacting. By going through this process on each project, we are laying a path to tell that story. We will know what our community's aspirations are and how to address their needs in the best way possible. Being able to tell these stories enables us to get buy-in from our staff, our administration, and any library stakeholder. We will be able to demonstrate the library's impact in a memorable way rather than just saying that a lot of people attended our outreach.

The design thinking process may initially sound like a lot of effort to put in for an outreach project. However, the design thinking exercises in this book (see chapter 6) can be done quickly and without spending much money. You will be able to test ideas through prototyping and piloting before spending a great deal of money on a final solution. Depending on the scope of your project and the size of your team, you may also choose to scale down or complete only some of the exercises (I've done these exercises with as few as two people, myself included). Once you become familiar with the mechanics behind these tools, it will be easy to determine which ones meet your particular needs.

The process and steps suggested in this book and in other design thinking resources are not meant to be strict paths to follow. Instead, they offer you the tools you need to reframe how you approach solving problems at your library. I use design thinking tools in all of my meetings to encourage staff to think creatively and to give everyone a voice in the process. Remember, at the end of the day, design thinking will help you to connect with your users and solve problems with intention.

TOOLS FOR HUMAN-CENTERED DESIGN

Remember, human-centered design is a way of thinking first. The tools are at the service of developing a new way of thinking about people and problems. While libraries value putting people first, we often design programs based on assumptions about what we think our users want rather than actually speaking to and observing them to find out what they really need. This can still lead to quality programming for the community, but it likely will also leave gaps in our services. Sometimes what we think the community wants is not what it needs.

The exercises provided in chapter 6 are only a small sampling of the multitude available to your library. IDEO released *Design Thinking for Libraries: A Toolkit for Patron-Centered Design* in conjunction with Chicago Public Library and Aarhus Public Libraries (in Denmark). The guide can be freely accessed online at http://designthinkingforlibraries.com. This robust guidebook includes a plethora of techniques and tools to get your library using design thinking on every project.

The LUMA Institute, a human-centered design instructional company, also has a great set of tools available for use on any project. You can purchase LUMA's book, *Innovating for People: Handbook of Human-Centered Design Methods*, through the institute's website at www.luma-institute.com.

Performing a search online for design thinking or human-centered design tools will also return a myriad of options. There are many great online workshops and videos that are useful for training in the different techniques available. Try lots of tools to see which ones work for your library.

ELEMENTS OF DESIGN THINKING

Putting People First

One of the most central elements of design thinking is designing programming based on the actual needs of stakeholders. You have to learn to empathize with the people who will be impacted by the services you are providing.

This means first identifying who all the potential stakeholders may be and then connecting with them directly. Look beyond just focus groups, interviews, and surveys. When planning technology-based outreach, it's also vital to understand how people interact with and use the technology you're planning to bring out of the library. Host observation sessions during which you watch how people use the technology you are interested in bringing out of the library. It is often the case that people will use things in ways they were not intended to be used.

Putting people first is more than just seeking input about what their needs are or how they interact with technology. This element of design thinking acknowledges that it is not just library experts who can solve a problem and provides the opportunity to bring on board more than just library staff to solve a problem. Inviting members of the community who will be served by your outreach to participate in its planning can be a great benefit to the project team as outside opinions will expand the creative output, leading to a more diverse set of solutions. You will also gain the first cheerleaders for your program.

Failing Successfully

We live in a world where failure often brings shame. The common belief is that failure leaves no path to success; failure is something that successful people never do. If we have this unhealthy relationship with failure, we will hesitate to release a new program to the public. We will spend our time perfecting every detail, ensuring that nothing is missed. We will work from the assumption that if anything goes wrong when the program is opened to the public, then it's all over. The program was a failure and must be scrapped, and we will need to try something entirely new.

Design thinking offers freedom from this rigid ideology. Instead of being herded along singular paths to success, you learn how to fail quickly and cheaply, iterating and improving along the way. Through prototypes and pilots, you can try out new ideas without expending all your resources. You will learn prototyping and piloting exercises in chapter 6 that will help you to implement outreach programming, without having every detail refined. Going out into the world and trying something, evaluating its successes and failures, and then iterating is how you will get more out of doing less.

Brainstorming

Brainstorming always felt like a forced activity to me. Teachers feigned excitement about brainstorming activities, but they never really seemed to be something that stimulated the class's creativity circuits. Most of my life I thought that creative people were born that way. Some of us are creative and others are doomed to live a life of mediocrity and white walls. This way of thinking is still prominent throughout most workplaces and schoolyards. It wasn't until the past thirty years that design firms even began breaking free of this perspective. Today, these companies recognize that not only can people other than designers design but anyone can be creative on cue rather than only when inspiration strikes.

In order to flex those creative muscles, you need to provide the proper stimulation. Walk into a staff meeting and tell everyone to start brainstorming, and you will likely hear groans. Yet, one of the most valuable techniques design thinking brings to library programming is engaged, productive brainstorming. You can utilize exercises to draw creative thoughts out of people. Understanding how to frame questions and using formulaic structures turns brainstorming into a game of sorts. Through design thinking, brainstorming becomes much more than someone standing at a whiteboard scribbling down anything someone yells out. Instead, it becomes a dynamic and fun process that brings to the surface many creative solutions to problems.

The brainstorming exercises used in human-centered design also give a voice to staff who may feel uncomfortable speaking up in a group of people. Utilizing these tools gives everyone an equal chance to be heard; all ideas are of value. The exercises I have learned from studying design thinking have reframed my approach to all brainstorming sessions. Although I often use the exercises exactly as they are written in chapter 6, I sometimes just use their key elements to transform any meeting into a creative endeavor.

Creative Thinking

One of the best things about being given the freedom to fail is that the constraint of feasibility is lifted. Because we can prototype ideas in a safe environment, we can experiment with solutions that may initially seem far-fetched, out of reach, or even fantastical. Giving staff this creative freedom to build out solutions to their ultimate fantasy is not only fun but also can showcase key elements that can be put into the final product.

A great example of this is when we at San José Public Library were designing our mobile makerspace, the Maker[Space]Ship. We worked with a group of teenagers to design the vehicle. When it came time for them to present their design, they showcased a bus with quite the presence. Before the Maker[Space]Ship approached its parking spot, you would first see a swarm of drones. Then, you would hear Richard Wagner's "Ride of the Valkyries" blaring from speakers. This is when you would catch sight of the brightly colored bus. As the bus parked, the swarm of drones would land on a platform attached to the roof. Suddenly, the back of the bus would fold down, smoke billowing out, and the librarians would walk out of the bus ready for some awesome science programs. What a thrilling sight to behold!

However, this level of decadence was not quite feasible on our budget. What we gathered from listening to this pitch was that the teens desired a vehicle that was out of this world. They wanted something with a presence, a vehicle that made you say, "Wow!" The final design took this into account, creating a bus with a vibrant exterior wrap and speakers on the outside, though there are no smoke machines yet. By using an unrestricted creative design process, we were able to pull out core themes and turn them into practical solutions.

NOTES

1. Jo Szczepanska, "Design Thinking Origin Story Plus Some of the People Who Made It All Happen," *Medium*, January 3, 2017, https://medium.com/@szczpanks/design-thinking-where-it-came-from-and-the-type-of-people-who-made-it-all-happen-dc3a05411e53.

2. Michael Ben-Eli, "Design Science: A Framework for Change" (New York: The Sustainability Institute, 2007), The Buckminster Fuller Institute, accessed June 14, 2018, www.bfi.org/design-science/primer/design-science-framework-change.

3. Yngve Sundblad, "UTOPIA: Participatory Design from Scandinavia to the World," in *IFIP Advances in Information and Communication Technology*, vol. 350, ed. J. Impagliazzo, P. Lundin, and B. Wangler (Berlin, Heidelberg: Springer, 2011) and *History of Nordic Computing* 3 (2010), 177.

4. Susanne Bødker, Pelle Ehn, Dan Sjögren, and Yngve Sundblad. "Co-operative Design— Perspectives on 20 Years with 'the Scandinavian IT Design Model,'" In *Proceedings of NordiCHI 2000* (Stockholm, Sweden: Royal Institute of Technology, 2000), 1.

5

BEST PRACTICES FOR DESIGN

What has your experience been with design thinking? Many people's only interaction with human-centered design is from a workshop at a conference that ends in a fun prototyping session. The presenters bust out the Play-Doh and pipe cleaners and instead of listening to a lecture, participants get the opportunity to experiment and play. It is a great conference exercise, something that gets people engaged in the process. However, by this point in the book, you may be asking yourself, "How in the world is this design thinking stuff going to be useful to me in my day-to-day life at the library?"

You likely are not alone in thinking that these tools are too abstract or that building things with pipe cleaners, though fun at a conference, will never be considered "real work" at your library. I, too, was one of these thinkers at the beginning of my exposure to human-centered design. I saw its potential in brainstorming exercises but not for anything beyond that. Now, I use these techniques to develop and plan every major project I manage in the library. In chapter 8, the case studies section of this book, you will read about real-world outreach programs that utilized design thinking in their creation and implementation.

Libraries are the perfect place to use design thinking. First, as librarians, we already desire to put our users first. The profit we are after is an increase in access and knowledge in the community. Learning the elements of design thinking and becoming comfortable with a variety of exercises gives us a skill set for doing just that.

Second, libraries are accountable to the public. We operate our libraries using public funds, which demands our good stewardship of that money. Working with technology projects can often be stalled due to a fear of failing and wasting public monies. Design thinking gives us a way to try out new services using very little money, learn from our mistakes, and adapt as we go. Using design thinking also gives us the means to respond to our environment quickly and efficiently. Neighborhoods are in a constant state of flux, and technology is changing even more rapidly. As we become more comfortable with the design thinking process, we will find ourselves becoming more flexible, able to meet the needs of our communities as they change.

You have taken the first step toward breaking free of the library walls and bringing technology-based outreach into your community by picking up this book. Design thinking can give you the framework to build your outreach plan. Many of the techniques and tools you will find in this book come from IDEO (www.ideo.com), Stanford's d.school (https://dschool.stanford .edu), and the LUMA Institute (www.luma-institute.com). However, hundreds of different tools are available for your library to use throughout the design process. Resources to find some of these tools can be found at the end of this book, and an Internet search will provide you with many more.

Human-centered design is an iterative process. You begin with identifying stakeholders and researching the community. Then, you define the problem you're trying to solve, develop solutions to the problem, test, fail, iterate, succeed, and evaluate. If at any point along this path, you see something not working or discover new and pertinent information, it is always okay to take a step backward and revisit previous exercises. Take time to reassess throughout the process to make sure that the next step on the path is where you need to be. Go back and repeat previous tools as needed. Do not feel confined to always be moving forward on the outlined path.

SET ASIDE THE SOLUTION

It seems natural to start a project with a defined solution already in place. Perhaps your library has decided to bring 3-D printers to the local elementary school during lunch periods. Although you may be energized to jump right into doing the outreach, starting with the solution does not address the problem your library is trying to solve. Use the design thinking process to take a step back from the solution in order to identify the larger problem. The solution you reach at the end of this process may be the same as what you began with, but the technology outreach will be grounded in insights derived from the community. These insights will enable you to evaluate your outreach efforts with a deeper understanding of what is working, moving beyond using only the number of people in attendance to gauge success.

BUILD A TOOLKIT

Before you start down the design thinking path, it is a good idea to build yourself a supply toolkit (e.g., see figure 5.1). These are some of the more common toolkit items:

> Sticky notes—of all sizes
> Sharpies or other markers
> Blank pieces of paper
> Colored construction paper

FIGURE 5.1 **Design Thinking Toolkit**

> Pipe cleaners
> Tape
> Play-Doh
> Scissors
> Binder clips
> Paper clips
> Assorted odds and ends (e.g., thread spools, straws, buttons, fabric scraps, coffee cups)

The items listed here are not required (though sticky notes are utilized heavily); they are suggestions of items that are often used in exercises. Having a toolkit readily available will enable you to jump right into a design thinking exercise whenever the mood strikes. Adapt your toolkit as you see fit!

Everyone is an artist. Many techniques in this book call upon you to put ideas down on sticky notes. It is highly encouraged that you draw your ideas! Stick figures and simple sketches are 100 percent acceptable. The brain processes visual information differently from written words. Seeing a board full of sticky notes dense with text can be visually overwhelming and make it difficult to immediately distinguish one idea from another. Simple drawings allow your team to look at a lot of ideas all at once, quickly noting their differences and similarities.

FOLLOW THE RULES OF BRAINSTORMING

Before beginning any of the design thinking exercises, it is important to learn the rules of brainstorming:

1. Defer judgment
2. Encourage wild ideas
3. Build on the ideas of others
4. Stay focused on the topic
5. One conversation at a time
6. Be visual
7. Go for quantity[1]

Ensure that all of your staff understand and practice these guidelines during any of the exercises found in this book or anytime you are participating in the design thinking process. You may even find it helpful to write these rules on a large sticky note and hang it in the room during each of your meetings.

RECORD THE DESIGN STORY

As you move through the design process, you will find that your team has created a great deal of artifacts. Make sure that you have thought about how to record and archive all the work you are creating. Many parts of this journey can be used later to tell the story of your work to stakeholders. Our library will often use prototypes to tell the story of our program's impact to potential funders.

You will also want to record all the different ideas you generate so that you can return to any point along this path and iterate. The design process is not a straight line; rather, you will move forward and backward, continually building upon the new information you have learned in one stage. Our teams like to take a lot of photos, and we often save the documents and prototypes people create during design sessions.

You will start your design journey by looking inward at the aspirations for your technology-based outreach and what barriers might prevent you from achieving those goals. Then, you will define your problem through a broad "How might we . . . ?" statement. Next, you will map out all your stakeholders, seeing who will be impacted by this new service. After that, you will gain insights into what your stakeholder needs, wants, and desires are through community interviews and observations. Then, your team will brainstorm solutions to the problem and prototype those solutions. Last, you'll pilot the program and gather feedback for evaluation and iteration.

IDENTIFY CONSTRAINTS

At this point, your team should not have any specifics about what your outreach will look like. It is perfectly acceptable for your team to start the design process with nothing more in mind than that they want to do technology outreach of some kind. Use the beginning of your first meeting to discuss some basics. Here are some questions to ask to get started:

1. What users are staff interested in serving through technology-based outreach?

2. Are there neighborhoods or specific places that we would like to do outreach?

3. Is there a specific piece of technology we would like to utilize at an outreach?

Answering these questions will help you define a very basic set of circumstances to start working with. You won't be defining the problem you are trying to solve quite yet, but you will be able to move forward with authority.

NOTE

1. "Effective Brainstorming Techniques," IDEO U, accessed June 14, 2018, www.ideou.com/pages/brainstorming.

DESIGN THINKING EXERCISES

A Path to Creative Problem Solving

You have built a toolkit and know the rules of brainstorming inside and out. Now it is time to start working with the design thinking exercises. You can follow the path outlined here with the exercises in the order presented, or you can alter the arrangement of the exercises to fit your project needs. As you practice these exercises, you will begin to see which ones are best suited for eliciting creative problem solving.

> **At the beginning, try following the guide as presented in this book.** Work through all of the exercises multiple times to become familiar with how they operate. Practice breeds familiarity and confidence.

THE EXERCISES

What are your aspirations and barriers?

❯ Aspirations and Barriers

What problems are you trying to solve?

❯ Problem Statement—Asking "How might we . . . ?"

Who are your stakeholders?

❯ Stakeholder Mapping

How do you gain insights from stakeholders?

- Empathizing
- Interviews
- Focus Groups
- Surveys
- Observation
- Feedback Boards
- Design Workshops

How do you review feedback from stakeholders?

- Empathy Maps

How do you brainstorm solutions?

- Mind Maps
- Creative Matrix
- Storyboards

How do you decide which solutions to prototype?

- Rapid Voting
- Decision Matrix

How do you anticipate surprises?

- Rose, Thorn, Bud

How can you try out solutions to your problem?

- Rapid Prototyping
- Act It Out
- Cover Story Mockup

How do you turn prototypes into real-world outreach programs?

- Piloting Outreach Programs

How do you know if the outreach is working?

- Deciding What to Evaluate
- Logic Models

What tools can you use for evaluation?

❯ Writing Surveys

....

Although the exercises of this chapter may seem like a lot, none of them take very long to complete. You might break the exercises into separate meetings, tackling small chunks of the project each time you gather. Alternately, you may choose to do longer sessions and perform many exercises at once. Due to the engaging nature of design thinking, hosting a two- or three-hour initial planning meeting has never drawn any complaints from staff. A good meeting schedule for planning might look like this:

Meeting 1 (2 hours)

> ❭ Aspirations and barriers
> ❭ Problem statement
> ❭ Stakeholder mapping
> ❭ Gaining insights plan (whom to speak with, how to reach them, and what to ask)

Between Meetings 1 and 2

> ❭ Gaining insights (interviews, surveys, feedback boards, observation, and/or design workshops)

Meeting 2 (1 hour)

> ❭ Empathy mapping
> ❭ Brainstorming solutions (mind maps, creative matrix, and/or storyboarding)
> ❭ Choosing solutions (rapid voting and/or decision matrix)
> ❭ Anticipating surprises (Rose, Thorn, Bud)

Meeting 3 (2 hours)

> ❭ Prototyping solutions (rapid prototyping, act it out, cover story mockup)
> ❭ Pilot program planning
> ❭ Evaluation planning

WHAT ARE YOUR ASPIRATIONS AND BARRIERS?

Aspirations are the hopes we hold close to us. We all have aspirations for the communities we serve, for our own professional development, and for our friends and family. Identify aspirations early on in crafting a technology-based outreach so that everyone on the project shares common ground. Think of aspirations as what your hopes and dreams are for a technology-based outreach service model at your library. Be lofty and bold; think broadly. The ideas you brainstorm here may transfer over to many different types of outreach. I often put the sticky notes derived from this exercise on a large piece of paper and hang it in my office to bring to future team meetings. Every time our team members meet, they are able to look at those sticky notes and be reminded of our shared aspirations. This helps to fuel inspiration, especially in moments when you may be stuck in the weeds.

Focusing only on all the potential benefits of your amazing new technology-based outreach program can be tempting. However, it's important that you also draw attention to the barriers that you may have to overcome in order to be successful. Again, when brainstorming barriers in this stage, think big. You will have time to hone in on specifics during the Rose, Thorn, Bud exercise later in this chapter. For now, invite your team members to think about all of the things that might block them from achieving their aspirations. Consider things that might go wrong or obstacles you may face along the way.

❯ ASPIRATIONS AND BARRIERS

SUPPLIES

> Sticky notes
> Whiteboard or large sheets of paper
> Markers

SETUP

1. Write "Aspirations" on one piece of paper or section of the whiteboard. Write "Barriers" on another piece of paper or the other half of the whiteboard.
2. Hand out markers and sticky notes.

STEPS

1. Set a timer for five minutes. Instruct staff to write down and/or draw the aspirations they have for a technology-based outreach program. Tell them not to get into program specifics quite yet but to think broadly.

2. Encourage staff to say their ideas out loud when they place them on the board. This can elicit other ideas that build upon the initial thoughts. Think, "Yes . . . , and . . ." rather than "No . . . , but . . ."

3. After five minutes, review the aspirations together. Ask, "What surprises you?" and "Do you notice any common themes?"

4. Repeat steps 1 through 3 for the barriers section. Again, tell team members to think broadly about what stumbling blocks might prevent your library from achieving their stated aspirations.

5. Keep the aspirations and barriers posted on the wall during the following "How might we . . . ?" exercise.

WHAT PROBLEM ARE YOU TRYING TO SOLVE?

At the start of any project, we have a problem that needs solving. Many times we begin developing an outreach plan without first identifying what the problem is that we are trying to solve. Instead, we begin with a neat idea. Your library may have been approached by a local business about setting up an outreach program at its location or know of a regular event that draws in big crowds. Libraries often see these opportunities and are quick to jump right in, filling a table with calendars and fliers about services and programs. Although there is great value in these awareness-based outreach events, they are mostly focused on solving one problem: people not being informed about library services. These "quick and dirty" outreach efforts are great at educating people about what the library has to offer and their success can be measured through simple metrics, including how many people visited the library's information table. When we begin moving into more complicated outreach programs that have specific learning objectives, it is vital for us to have clarity and direction about the problem we are attempting to solve.

Taking a step back and approaching your outreach through defining the problem give your team an immense amount of power. You will no longer

This exercise (like all others) can be moved around based on the order in which you complete it. After defining aspirations and barriers, you may choose to map out stakeholders and then perform community interviews, coming back to define the problem after gathering more information about your community's needs. Try switching the order of operations for these exercises to find what works best for your team and the problem you are trying to solve.

just be executing an outreach plan; rather, you will be working toward achieving the aspirations your team identified in the previous exercise. The problem statement you create in this next exercise will be broad enough to explore and build many different technology-based outreach programs. As you evaluate and iterate, you can use the problem statement to drive future innovations.

This stage of the process is the most critical but also can be incredibly challenging. You may be used to tackling problems by focusing on the technology you have available to you or the end-service goal. Instead, in this exercise, you will be taking a look at your broader objectives and goals. Have the aspirations and barriers posted on the wall while your team is defining your problem. Keeping the work you create throughout the exercises available for the team to see during the planning process aids staff in the iterative cycle of design thinking. Looking back at where you have been is always helpful in seeing the path forward.

During this exercise, your team will define a problem statement or, as it is most commonly referred to in design thinking circles, a "How might we . . . ?" question. Considering "How might we . . . ?" will be the guiding force in helping you to make design decisions for your project. Your question should be "broad enough for creative freedom . . . [but] narrow enough to make it manageable."[1]

For example, if you ask, "How might I build a mobile makerspace?" the outcome would be building a mobile makerspace. Once it was built, you would have met that singular goal and be left with no metrics for evaluating success. Steer away from questions that focus on the implementation of the solution. A better question for the mobile makerspace project is, "How might we inspire creative problem solving?" Asking this question opens many avenues for creativity. One possible solution might be building a physical mobile makerspace, but you now have a problem statement that can drive decisions about what activities people do on board, the places the outreach will happen, the design of the bus itself, and so forth.

Asking "How might we . . . ?" touches all aspects of the outreach effort. This is an important step, but don't feel married to your initial problem statement. Again, design thinking is a flexible process. You may discover after gaining insights from your community through surveys and interviews that your initial problem statement does not quite fit anymore. Go back to revisit it often, and do not be afraid to update it to fit your current set of needs.

> **Start each planning meeting by reading the problem statement aloud.** Ask team members if they think it is still the problem they should be solving. If not, take time to return to this exercise to write a new "How might we . . . ?" question.

❯ PROBLEM STATEMENT— ASKING "HOW MIGHT WE . . . ?"

SUPPLIES

> Markers
> Sticky notes
> Whiteboard or large sheet of paper
> Small stickers of any shape or color (enough for everyone to have two)

SETUP

1. Write "How might we . . . ?" on a whiteboard or large piece of paper.
2. If possible, have the aspirations and barriers from the previous exercise on display in the room.
3. If you have completed other exercises before this one, such as community interviews or a stakeholder map, post those on the wall as well.
4. Hand out sticky notes and markers.

STEPS

1. In this exercise, you want team members to think broadly. As an example, tell them not to ask questions like, "How might I buy a car?" but instead ask, "How might I get from school, to work, to home?"

2. Give the team five minutes to brainstorm "How might we . . . ?" questions. Remind them that these should be broad statements that define the problem you are trying to solve.

3. After five minutes, give team members a chance to put their questions on the board, saying them aloud as they do.

4. Discuss the problem statements, grouping similar ideas together by moving the sticky notes.

5. Hand out two stickers to each person. Tell everyone to vote for their favorite statements. They can put two stickers on the same one if it suits their fancy. Have everyone vote at the same time to discourage follow-the-leader behavior. You will find more information about this process in the Rapid Voting exercise later in this chapter.

6. Write the top three to five problem statements on the whiteboard.

7. As a group, talk about what you like about each of the statements. Can they be combined? Does one stand out for the group right away? Feel free to start writing new statements on the board during the discussion, refining together until you come up with a "How might we . . . ?" question of which the whole group approves.

Remember, the problem statement you come up with is not cemented in place for all time. As you move through the design thinking process, you may discover that it needs to be updated based on new insights. That's okay! At the beginning of every team meeting, refer back to the statement to make sure everyone is still comfortable with it and its goals moving forward, and adjust as needed.

WHO ARE YOUR STAKEHOLDERS?

Before we solve any problems or develop any outreach programs, we have to look at who our stakeholders are going to be. Who will be impacted by implementing this outreach? The services we provide are not insular. The people we target directly are not the only ones affected by our programs. Stakeholders can be both internal and external. Do not fall into the trap of considering only current library patrons. Your staff will be impacted, as will the people in the neighborhood where you set up shop; government departments or other community organizations can also be connected to the work that you do. This exercise will assist you in thinking about all the layers of people who are impacted by your technology-based outreach.

Remember, humans are front and center in this design process. The input we gather from our stakeholders drives our design process. We have to be able to empathize with these people, connecting with them to make sure that our solution is what they actually need, not just what we assume they want. This is even more important when doing technology outreach which has the potential to be more expensive than traditional models and which presents many more opportunities for things to go wrong. We want to know that users are in need of this solution—that it is something that will positively impact their lives while serving the library's mission— before we spend our money.

Stakeholder mapping is a technique best used during your first working session with your team, which could include anywhere from two people, for a small library or project, to a large number of staff from many different departments. Beginning a project by drawing attention to the stakeholders gets everyone focused on the right target audiences from the get-go. Because you are starting with a broad problem statement, creating a stakeholder map is an essential step that gives you your first chance to narrow your focus and establish a safe place to begin a discussion around the goals for the project.

As part of the mapping process, your team will identify three different groups of stakeholders: indirect, direct, and core. Indirect stakeholders are people who may touch the project peripherally; examples include a person who is not attending your program but faces a longer commute time due to increased traffic at an event and staff in your IT department who may have to take a service call when the Wi-Fi goes down at an event. Identifying these stakeholders keeps you aware of their needs, but they are not the people you are designing for directly.

The direct stakeholder group includes individuals whom the program will touch on a deeper level but who are still not the main audience for the outreach. Members of this group often have a connection to someone in the core stakeholder group; examples include parents of children in the core group or staff members who have to handle an increase in technology-related reference questions at the branch after each outreach. Pay special attention to this group when designing your programs because it may include the gatekeepers to future learning or those making decisions about who will attend the outreach.

Last are the core stakeholders, who are those for whom we are designing our program services. This group of stakeholders will be impacted the most by our outreach efforts. It is fine to identify several different groups as potential core stakeholders. As you move into brainstorming solutions to your problem, you may choose to narrow your focus onto just one of the core groups or try to meet the needs of various stakeholders in one program.

After completing your stakeholder map, you will have developed a list of people with whom you will want to connect. The next stage will involve speaking with those people, observing their behaviors, and gaining insights into their needs.

❯ STAKEHOLDER MAPPING

SUPPLIES

> ❯ Sticky notes
> ❯ Markers
> ❯ Whiteboard or large sheet of paper

SETUP

1. Draw a large circle on the whiteboard. Label this circle "Indirect."
2. Draw a smaller circle inside of the first circle. Label this circle "Direct."
3. Draw an even smaller circle inside the second circle. Label this circle "Core."
4. Hand out sticky notes and markers.

STEPS

1. Explain to your team that in this exercise they will be thinking about who is going to be impacted by the technology-based outreach.

2. Set a timer for five minutes. Ask the team to brainstorm as many different stakeholders as possible, including both internal and external.

3. Have team members draw or write stakeholders on the sticky notes and put the notes in the appropriate circles on the whiteboard.

4. Tell everyone to try to come up with at least one stakeholder for each circle.

5. At the end of the brainstorm, review the sticky notes together. Group together sticky notes with similar stakeholders.

6. Discuss the findings. Did anyone put the same stakeholder in different circles? Ask whether anyone disagrees with the placement of a stakeholder. Try to reach a consensus for stakeholder placement.

HOW DO YOU GAIN INSIGHTS FROM STAKEHOLDERS?

Now that your team has finished the stakeholder map, you have an idea of who will be the people directly affected by your outreach. During this exercise, you will begin developing a list of the people your team will want to interview, observe, and/or pull into your team to work on solving the problem that you identified earlier. Plan to connect with someone from each of the stakeholder groups listed in the core circle and also with a good sampling of people from the direct group. Speaking to at least one or two people from the indirect group may also be helpful but is not always necessary.

❯ EMPATHIZING

Once you have identified the stakeholders who will be impacted by your outreach, it is time to connect with them, to empathize. The problems we try to solve are very rarely our own, and because of that, we have to put ourselves in our stakeholders' shoes; we have to have empathy for them, gaining an understanding of what is important to them. This is a good time to use the tools presented in "Turning Outward Resources for Libraries" from the Harwood Institute,[2] if you haven't already. Your team may have already gathered some insights from the broader community as part of your neighborhood assessment (see chapter 2). You now need to focus more directly, connecting with your stakeholders to discuss what they need from a technology-based outreach program.

The techniques found in this section are mostly performed outside of your team meetings. However, you will work together to decide which of these methods to employ and brainstorm the types of questions to ask stakeholders. It is not necessary to perform all of the exercises found in this section of the chapter. One of the most exhilarating aspects of design thinking is that you get to choose your own adventure. Your staff may find that one-on-one interviews are the perfect choice for one type of stakeholder, but that feedback boards work much better with a different group. Try out lots of different ways of connecting! There is no singular right way. Also, remember that failure is how you learn. If one of these methods does not work in your library, take time to figure out what went wrong. There will be more opportunities to try it again or move on to something different.

The size of your library and scale of your project will determine the exhaustiveness of the methods that you need to use to gain insights from the community. For large projects, you may have identified many different stakeholder groups. As such, more time and resources will need to be spent reaching out to those people. Although it may feel like an easy step to gloss over, gaining insight from the people who will be impacted by your project is critical to developing successful technology-based outreach programs. In the process of speaking to and observing people, your team may also discover other areas of service outside your immediate purview. This new information can help you to create more robust outreach models or expand services into other areas.

❱ INTERVIEWS

Interviews ask targeted and focused questions of a defined set of stakeholders. You might choose to interview people after observing them or it could be an entirely independent venture. Either way, you will want to come prepared with a list of questions. These questions should be formatted in such a way as to elicit thoughtful answers, rather than simply yes or no responses.

SUPPLIES
> Interview questions
> Markers

> Note-taking tools (paper and pen, laptop, and/or recording device)
> Whiteboard or large sheet of paper

SETUP

1. Identify which stakeholders to interview. Use the stakeholder map you created earlier to determine with whom you will want to speak. The amount of time and resources your library has at its disposal will be part of the decision-making process when you decide which stakeholders and how many from each group to interview. At the very least, plan on speaking to five to ten individuals. The core stakeholder group will be the most critical audience to interview.

2. Write a list of all the different stakeholder categories from which you plan on interviewing people. Then, identify how you can reach out and secure interviews with individuals. Where do people from this stakeholder group congregate? Are you able to meet them where they are? You will need to connect with the stakeholder groups to schedule interview times with individuals. Finally, brainstorm the pathways to connect with the stakeholders you want to interview.

3. Assign different team members to perform the interviews. Ideally, interviews are performed in teams of two: an interviewer and a note taker. The interviewer can remain focused on asking questions, alleviating tensions that can be experienced by the interviewee. Many people get nervous during interviews. This can be heightened if the interviewer is constantly looking down to write notes. Remove this stressor through the use of a dedicated note taker or a recording device if a second person isn't available to assist with the interview.

4. Give team members a deadline by which to complete the interviews. Staff are then responsible

> **Perform the steps** for developing interview questions even if your group is not planning on doing interviews. The exercise will inform your work for feedback boards, surveys, and focus groups.

for scheduling and performing the interviews outside of meeting times.

5. As a group, brainstorm interview questions to ask different stakeholders. Assign one person to write the questions on the whiteboard. Questions should elicit knowledge about the stakeholder group and inform the problem you are trying to solve.

> **Here are some rules for conducting a good interview:**
>
> 1. Be prepared with questions and recording equipment.
> 2. Introduce yourself and explain the purpose of the interview.
> 3. Obtain consent.
> 4. Start with simple questions.
> 5. Take good notes.
> 6. Be attentive.

6. Move through the completed question list one by one. Write down which stakeholders should be asked each question. Don't fall into the trap of asking every stakeholder the same questions.

7. Compile the final lists of interview questions for each of the stakeholder groups. Keep interviews relatively short. Limit interviews to no more than ten questions or thirty minutes.

8. Distribute the appropriate lists to the team members who will be conducting the interviews with the stakeholder groups.

STEPS

1. Plan on speaking with three to five people from each stakeholder group. Team members are responsible for making arrangements to hold interviews with their preassigned stakeholder groups. They may choose to interview one person at a time or hold small-group conversations. For more details on interviewing small groups, see the following Focus Groups section.

2. Secure a room that has enough space for everyone attending and where you can be undisturbed for the length of the interview.

3. Provide incentives for coming to an interview. Inexpensive gift cards are a great motivator to offer participants. In my experience, a five-dollar gift card for coffee gets people in the door far more often than offering nothing. If money is not available in your

project budget, connect with your library friends group or ask for donations from local businesses. I have even offered a reduction in fines to people who volunteered their time as part of an interview or focus group.

4.   Perform the interview.

5.   Meet immediately with the note taker, if there is one, after the interview to discuss your findings. Add any additional observations you had that the note taker did not write down. If you worked solo, listen to the recording shortly after and write down notes.

6.   Get those sticky notes out and draw pictures with short phrases to capture the insights from the interviews. Gather notes into themes that can be expressed back to the team at the next meeting.

❯ FOCUS GROUPS

Focus groups are similar to interviews. Instead of speaking with individuals one-on-one, the interviewer for a focus group connects with many people at once. This is useful if you have identified a stakeholder group that meets together on a regular basis. In the past, I have done focus groups with teen volunteers and ESL (English as a second language) classes. An engaged audience that already comes to the library can be easier to access than individuals for interviews.

Follow the instructions listed in the previous Interviews exercise for planning and executing your focus groups. However, instead of reaching out to individuals, connect with preestablished groups. You can also hold focus groups with stakeholders who do not already meet as a group. If your team goes this route, you will need to advertise the event. Instead of offering individuals gift cards as incentives, provide snacks for those who attend.

Keep an eye out for participants in focus groups who dominate the discussion. If you notice only one or two people speaking, it is okay to thank them for their input and then ask one or more other participants some direct questions. Make sure everyone has a chance to speak.

❯ SURVEYS

Surveys are another avenue for collecting stakeholder input. They are useful when you have large groups of stakeholders to gather information from or a stakeholder group that regularly comes into your library. The two main types of surveys are paper and digital. Consider the audience group you are trying to reach when creating the survey. If the group has limited access to computers and the Internet, a paper survey may prove to be more effective than its digital counterpart.

SUPPLIES

> Online survey or paper surveys

SETUP

1. Determine which stakeholder groups to reach through surveys.
2. Decide which questions you want to include in the survey. You may choose to use the same questions that your team brainstormed in the Interviews exercise or come up with some new ones.
3. Begin with the simplest questions. This will ease people into the survey. Include a mix of open- and closed-ended questions. If you are gauging interest in a particular area, such as how comfortable someone is with technology, consider including questions with a ranking scale. Different stakeholder groups may require their own unique sets of questions. Evaluate which questions should be asked of every participant and which questions should be posed to only certain groups.
4. Discuss the merits of having paper versus online surveys. Which will be most effective with the groups you're trying to reach? It is possible that a mix of both digital and paper surveys will work best for some groups.

If your team decides that paper surveys are the best format for gathering your information, creating a digital survey for data collection is still a useful endeavor. Staff can input answers from the paper surveys collected into the digital version.

5. Even if performing paper surveys, build an online survey for later input of the data collected.
6. Print surveys, if required.

STEPS

1. Reach out to stakeholder groups to distribute surveys. This may be done through in-person contact, handing out paper forms, or through a link to the online survey. Consider reaching out using the library's social media accounts or e-mail newsletters if you are trying to gain lots of responses from a diverse group of stakeholders.

> **Many online survey** tools are available for libraries to use. The three most commonly used are SurveyMonkey, Google Forms, and SurveyGizmo.

2. Collect paper surveys.
3. Input paper survey results into the online survey.
4. Review survey data for broad themes and specifics that stand out. Bring these findings back to your next team meeting.

❯ OBSERVATION

Observation is one of the easiest ways to gain insights into a group of stakeholders. Through observation, you can learn the ways in which someone interacts with technology before you leave the library and bring that technology to your community. Asking people how they plan to or currently use a tool only gives one piece of the puzzle. Instead, you need to look at the big picture by observing people in their natural habitat, seeing how they interact with the tools in their environment. You can get people's perceptions of what they want to do with technology through an interview, but observation allows you to look behind the curtain. Observation opens up doors to new knowledge by revealing how people actually use tools rather than just relying on how people say they intend to use them.

SUPPLIES

> Note-taking tools (paper and pen or laptop)

SETUP

1. In your team meeting, decide on how and where you plan to observe stakeholders. Observation can take many different forms and should not involve just watching someone interact with the technology you plan on utilizing at your outreach. If you have already established where your outreach is going to be, send staff to observe how stakeholders interact with the location. If you already know that you will be using a particular piece of technology, try to observe how people use it. This could be done in your library or at another location.

2. Discuss if your observations will be passive or active. Active observation is when you invite a group of people to participate in the observation. You may give them the technology and watch them use it; they know they are being observed. Passive observation often takes place in a public space with the observer acting as a "fly on the wall."

3. Think about the specifics you will be looking for during the observation period. What errors do users experience? Did someone give up right away or troubleshoot? Did participants interact with the technology on their own or in groups? Did they use the technology as it was intended to be used?

STEPS

1. If your observations are going to be active, gain permission to observe the group. This might be a class at school or a specific group of people whom you've recruited. Explain to participants that you are going to be taking notes and watching how they go about their days or perform tasks.

2. Write detailed notes about what you observe. Include the facial expressions and body language you observe in addition to vocalizations. These nonverbal cues can give you just as much insight as what someone says aloud.

3. After the observation period, categorize notes into themes to share with team members at the follow-up meeting.

❯ FEEDBACK BOARDS

Sometimes the best method to reach a group of stakeholders is through feedback boards. A larger group of people can share their knowledge without having to commit much of their time. Some stakeholders may feel uncomfortable speaking one-on-one with library staff or do not want to be personally connected to the comments they are making.

Consider the placement of the feedback board. Will it reside in your computer room in order to engage current users of library technology? In the school cafeteria where you plan to host robotics competitions? At the senior center where you want to conduct e-book training? Feedback boards can also be made and posted digitally. If your stakeholder group has a strong presence online, post a question to your library's Facebook page or other social media account to elicit their feedback.

SUPPLIES

> Butcher paper, poster board, or other medium that provides space to write the question and gather responses
> Markers
> Sticky notes (can collect feedback on sticky notes or directly on the board)

SETUP

1. Determine which stakeholder groups to reach through a feedback board.
2. Look at the list of questions that were developed during the Interviews exercise. Select one of these questions for the board. It is important to select a question that people can answer in one to two sentences. Questions that involve lengthy stories are best left to interviewing.
3. Brainstorm possible locations for the board. If it is going to be posted outside the library, whom will staff need to contact in order to gain permission to implement the board?
4. Gather your supplies and write the question in large, easy-to-read letters at the top of the board. Leave space for participants to answer the question.

5. Stakeholders can respond directly on the feedback board or use sticky notes. Sticky notes encourage participants to respond with more brevity, as the size of the note allows only a certain amount of text or imagery.

6. Decide on a length of time for the feedback board to be active. This could be one day, perhaps at a large event, up to a few weeks or longer. Staff will need to monitor the board, removing sticky notes if it gets too full or replacing it with a clean board if there is no room left for comments, while the project is still active.

STEPS

1. Set up the feedback board in your desired location.

2. Train library staff on the reasoning behind the board. If the board is not being placed in your library, ensure that the staff members at that location understand its purpose and how people are supposed to use it.

3. Invite people to participate by answering the question.

4. At the end of the time period for the board, do an initial assessment of the responses. Write down any broad themes that can be shared back with the team. Keep any of the comments that stood out or revealed a big impact from the outreach. These stories can be used later for marketing endeavors.

❯ DESIGN WORKSHOPS

Another method of gathering information from stakeholders is through hosting design workshops. Some of the best ideas come from letting people play with how they would solve the problem you have identified. In the How Can You Try Out Solutions to Your Problems? section of this chapter, you will find several different techniques that can be used with various stakeholder groups. Identify a group of stakeholders to work with, much like you did for a focus group. Use the exercises in the prototyping section to direct participants in solving your problem.

While building San José Public Library's mobile makerspace, we invited a group of teens to a design workshop. The teens were given information from the interviews and worked in groups with staff to design the physical bus. Each team had supplies from the design thinking toolbox. One team drew the bus in tape on the wall, using sticky notes to identify different areas and tools inside. The other team utilized Play-Doh, pipe cleaners, and sticky notes to build the mobile makerspace. Aspects of both teams' designs ended up in the final, real-world vehicle.

HOW DO YOU REVIEW FEEDBACK FROM STAKEHOLDERS?

To truly gain insight, you need to have a review process in place to draw out the common themes you are seeing. By grouping commonalities together and identifying themes, the bigger picture will shine through all that data. The themes you find will tell you if people are saying the same things, using technology in the same ways, or demonstrating any complex issues that may require creating separate projects to meet all their needs.

After completing any of the gaining insights activities from the previous section, take time to reflect on what you heard and saw. Doing this within two days of performing the exercise ensures the material is still fresh in your mind. Take detailed notes to facilitate a thorough review of each session. Take a first pass at reading these notes or listening to the recordings and highlight items that stand out to you. Then, review the highlighted items on a second pass through. I will often do this second pass with my stack of trusty sticky notes in hand, writing or drawing (drawing is highly encouraged in this stage) themes I see or stand-alone items that will be of value to discuss with the project team.

Set aside time for note takers and interviewers to review their notes from the gaining insights exercises. When the team reconvenes, everyone can share their findings. Together, you can continue the process of identifying commonalities and themes. Instead of focusing on the minutiae from each exercise, you will begin to see the big impact areas.

Once the gaining insights exercises have been completed and facilitators have gotten a chance to review their notes, pulling out themes and important details, come back together as a project team. Place sticky notes up on the wall, calling attention to and naming the different themes. Have a discussion about the findings. These are some of the questions to cover during the team meeting:

> Are there commonalities across stakeholder groups? What differences do you notice?

> Did what people say match your assumptions?

> What was surprising?

> Has the connection with the community changed the way you are thinking about the potential outreach?

> Did people use technology in the way it was intended?

> What do people want to learn?

> What are the aspirations of each stakeholder group?

When you are observing people using technology, it can be more helpful to know how someone interacts with a device rather than if that device is being used correctly. If one person uses a piece of technology in a certain way but twenty people use it another way, it is more valuable to know what the twenty people did. The outlier is not indicative of the entire stakeholder group.

❯ EMPATHY MAPS

One of the best ways to help digest all the insights gained while connecting with the community is by creating an empathy map (see figure 6.1). Remember, the reason behind the entire process of gaining insights is to develop more empathy for the stakeholders. You want to understand how people feel, and be able to share in that feeling, in order to serve them efficiently and effectively. An empathy map lets you identify what matters most to different stakeholders: What are people . . .

> thinking and feeling?

> seeing?

> hearing?

> saying and doing?

In addition, you will need to brainstorm potential pain and gain points for stakeholders.

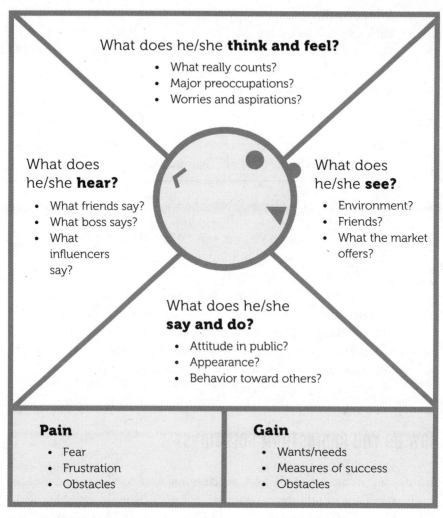

What does he/she think and feel?

- What really counts?
- Major preoccupations?
- Worries and aspirations?

What does he/she hear?

- What friends say?
- What boss says?
- What influencers say?

What does he/she see?

- Environment?
- Friends?
- What the market offers?

What does he/she say and do?

- Attitude in public?
- Appearance?
- Behavior toward others?

Pain

- Fear
- Frustration
- Obstacles

Gain

- Wants/needs
- Measures of success
- Obstacles

FIGURE 6.1 **Empathy Map Worksheet**

SUPPLIES

> Printed empathy maps or whiteboard
> Markers

SETUP

1.   Plan to complete an empathy map for each of the stakeholder groups you connected with through the gaining insights exercises.

2. Print empathy maps, enough so that each team has one copy for each stakeholder group.
3. Break into pairs or teams of three. Alternatively, if you have a small group, you can do the mapping together on a whiteboard.
4. Distribute the empathy maps and markers.

STEPS

1. Choose one stakeholder group to start with, and have all teams write the name in the center of their maps.
2. Explain to the teams that the stakeholder listed on the map is a representative persona of everyone from that group.
3. Move around the map from box to box, and have the teams fill in the details for each section. Ask, "What is this stakeholder thinking, feeling, seeing, hearing, saying, and doing?" and "What are the pain and gain points for this stakeholder?"
4. When everyone is done, have each team share its findings.
5. You may choose to create one master empathy map for each stakeholder group as the discussion proceeds. You can do this on another printed map or on a whiteboard (make sure to take a photo before wiping it clean for the next round).
6. Repeat this exercise for each stakeholder group.

HOW DO YOU BRAINSTORM SOLUTIONS?

By this stage in the process, your team has already done a lot to understand the needs of the community. You have gained insights by speaking with users and developed a problem statement. Now, you will use everything you have learned so far to brainstorm solutions to your problem. Many engaging tools, such as the ones described in this section, can help your team generate lots of ideas quickly. Feel free to use one or all of the following tools in your process. You can use them sequentially, with each building off the previous one, to create more detailed and defined solutions as you progress through each exercise.

This is not the time to put limits on yourself! Now is the time to flex those creative muscles. Do not feel confined to what is feasible. The solutions you brainstorm and prototype can go beyond the scope of realistic possibilities. Through prototyping them later on, you will discover elements that can be built into real-world outreach programs.

❯ MIND MAPS

A mind map is a hierarchical diagram that shows relationships. A problem statement, in this case your "How might we . . . ?" question, is placed in the middle of a piece of paper and solutions are drawn out from it like branches on a tree. You start with broad ideas and themes that will solve your problem, narrowing concepts into workable solutions as you continue branching off from the middle.

SUPPLIES
> Blank paper or whiteboard
> Markers
> Sticky notes

SETUP
1. Arrange the team members as appropriate. This activity can be done individually, in pairs, or as a group on a whiteboard.
2. Hand out paper and markers.

STEPS
1. Have everyone write your "How might we . . . ?" question in the middle of the paper and then draw a circle around the question.
2. Explain that everyone will generate solutions to the problem statement written in the middle of the paper, beginning with broad solution themes. Limit solutions to one word or short phrases that explain a concept (e.g., technology, outreach, classes), and

Each solution can have multiple branches coming off of it. Using the example in step 3, once you get to the instructional classes solution, you could narrow down that category to more audiences than just seniors, for example, teachers, children, or library staff.

demonstrate the approach for the team: Draw a line coming off the main question in the middle. Then, write the solution and draw an enclosure around it.

3. Keep on brainstorming solutions with the team, expanding the map by creating new branches. Explain that each new branch should define the solution in more detail, for example, technology → e-readers → instructional classes → seniors.

4. Give the team five minutes to complete the mind maps.

5. Have each team member share his or her mind map. Write down solutions on sticky notes. Write only one solution per sticky note.

6. Save these solutions for use in later exercises, such as the Decision Matrix.

❯ CREATIVE MATRIX

The creative matrix, my favorite way to spawn new ideas, is a powerhouse of idea creation, quickly generating a firestorm of solutions. You can consider potential service models and/or solution themes with specific stakeholder groups in mind, helping you to devise new ideas to solve your problem.

SUPPLIES

> Whiteboard or large sheet of paper
> Markers
> Sticky notes

SETUP

1. Draw a large grid with at least three rows and three columns of cells.

2. Label the columns with various stakeholders.

3. Label the rows as categories for enabling solutions. Consider using the solutions generated in the first branch of the Mind Maps exercise. Alternatively, use different types of technology or places being considered for the outreach.

4. Write your "How might we . . . ?" question at the top of the board.

5. Hand out sticky notes and markers to each person.

STEPS

1. Explain that this tool is for rapid idea generation. Ask each person to come up with at least one solution for each of the intersecting boxes on the matrix.

2. Give everyone five to ten minutes to brainstorm as many ideas as possible. Perform this step individually. Encourage everyone to write or draw their solutions on the sticky notes and place them in the appropriate intersecting boxes. Explain that it is okay to overlap other sticky notes as you will be doing a group share at the end.

3. At the end of the brainstorm, give each person an opportunity to share his or her ideas. Read through the sticky notes in each box. If there are similar ideas, group the sticky notes together.

4. If desired, at this stage you can start to narrow down solutions that the group likes. Use the Rapid Voting exercise (see next section) or come to consensus through discussion.

5. Save this exercise's solutions to use in later exercises, such as the Decision Matrix, Storyboards, or Rapid Prototyping.

❯ STORYBOARDS

Storyboards, much like any of the other tools in this book, can be used at different moments throughout the design process. You can use a storyboard for brainstorming, as described here, or as a prototyping exercise, later on in the design process, to flesh out solutions you developed in the Creative Matrix or Mind Maps exercises. I find storyboarding to be extremely helpful in unlocking new ideas; instead of just writing solutions on sticky notes, my team can express their ideas through drawing. This is your first opportunity to think about the details of a solution and tell the story of its potential impact. The visual nature of this exercise also means that storyboards are great tools for communicating the outreach plan to funders or any other library stakeholder.

SUPPLIES

> Large and small sticky notes
> Markers

> Small blank pieces of paper
> Three small containers to hold paper slips

SETUP

1. Before meeting with your team, create brainstorm generators on the blank pieces of paper. On the slips, write different potential outreach locations, stakeholder groups, and types of technology.
2. Put the slips into different containers, separating out the locations, stakeholders, and technology.
3. Separate your team into groups of two to four. Smaller teams can complete the exercise individually or as one group.
4. Have each group draw three brainstorm generators, one from each category.
5. Pass out sticky notes and markers.
6. If you have the space, invite teams to stick their storyboards to the wall before getting started. Standing up during a brainstorming activity gets those creative juices flowing.

STEPS

1. Instruct groups to divide their large sticky notes into nine boxes.
2. Have them write your "How might we . . . ?" question at the top of their papers.
3. Have group members draw a story of what the technology-based outreach looks like using the stakeholders, technology, and locations on their slips.
4. Give fifteen minutes for groups to draw their stories of the outreach, including a beginning, a middle, and an end.
5. Have groups share their storyboards one by one.
6. Hold a group discussion, encouraging questions.
7. Write down solutions that stand out on smaller sticky notes. Save these for use in later exercises, such as the Decision Matrix and Rapid Prototyping.

HOW DO YOU DECIDE WHICH SOLUTIONS TO PROTOTYPE?

Now that your team has generated a plethora of solutions to your "How might we . . . ?" question, how do you know which ones to explore in more detail through prototyping? None of us have the time or resources to dive deep into all the ideas our teams brainstorm. Two different methods you can use to figure out which ideas to move forward into the prototyping stage are rapid voting and the decision matrix.

❯ RAPID VOTING

If you want to pick out some solutions quickly, rapid voting is the perfect tool. It is fast, easy, and gives everyone a voice. This style of decision making removes the "follow the leader" instinct many groups have. Instead of team members holding back and waiting for one person to make a decision and then following that person's lead, they all cast their votes at the same time. You used the rapid voting process earlier during the Problem Statement (asking "How might we . . . ?") exercise, and you can use it as part of any exercise that involves narrowing down a pool of ideas.

SUPPLIES
  - › Small stickers (enough for everyone to have two)
  - › Solutions on sticky notes (five to ten ideas)

SETUP
  1. Hand out two stickers to each person.
  2. Choose five to ten solutions from the brainstorming exercises (Storyboards, Creative Matrix, and/or Mind Maps) and write them on the sticky notes. Place the sticky notes on a wall. Space out the ideas such that it is easy to identify them individually.

STEPS
  1. Read each of the ideas out loud so that everyone on the team knows what they are.
  2. Have everyone line up in front of the ideas.

3. Explain that when you say "Go," all team members should place their stickers on their favorite solutions. If they really love one idea, they can place all of their stickers on that one; they don't have to choose separate ideas.

4. Tally up the votes. Decide how many solutions you have the resource bandwidth to delve into more deeply. A good number to explore in prototyping is two to four ideas.

❯ DECISION MATRIX

Often after completing a brainstorming activity, you will have so many great solutions to your "How might we . . . ?" problem that it seems impossible to decide which ones to pursue. A decision matrix gives you a way to compare your solutions against one another based on two different data points. You can choose anything you want to put on the axes of the matrix. My favorite metrics are cost and difficulty. You may also choose other criteria such as importance, length of time, administration support, community engagement, or grant opportunities.

After completing the matrix once, you might want to repeat the exercise with new metrics to see whether different solutions stand out for you. Repeating this exercise is a great way to refine your solution pool, extracting the ideas that appear to hold the most value for your organization in terms of cost, importance to the strategic plan, or community engagement.

SUPPLIES

> Solutions on sticky notes (ten to twenty ideas)
> Whiteboard or large piece of paper

SETUP

1. Draw a horizontal line and a vertical line near the edges of the whiteboard to create a line graph.
2. Label each axis with the comparatives you selected.
3. Place the sticky notes in an easily accessible location for the group.

STEPS

1. As a group, place the sticky notes on the matrix according to where they fall based on the chosen metrics. If you have chosen

cost (y-axis) and difficulty (x-axis), then a solution that is very expensive but very easy to accomplish will be high on the y-axis and far left on the x-axis.

2. Once the group has placed all the sticky notes on the board, discuss their placement. Move ideas around if the discussion suggests they are better suited somewhere else in relation to another idea.

3. Select two to four ideas to move forward into prototyping. This could be a perfect time to use the Rapid Voting exercise! You may decide to move forward with only solutions that are easy and simple, or you may be okay forging ahead with difficult and expensive ideas. The decision matrix gives you a chance to see what it might take to accomplish one of the solutions, thereby allowing you to make a more informed choice about which to pursue in more detail.

HOW DO YOU ANTICIPATE SURPRISES?

No one likes unpleasant surprises. This is especially true if you have spent a lot of time and money on a project. It stings when no one shows up for the outreach you spent months planning or when you have a major technology failure on-site. Although you cannot anticipate everything, there is an exercise you can do to help identify possible opportunities, successes, and challenges. As with other design thinking exercises, this one will allow you to work smartly, preparing yourself and your team for possible challenges before spending your money and time on creating the actual outreach. In this exercise, called Rose, Thorn, Bud, you will use different-colored sticky notes to identify potential successes (roses), challenges (thorns), and opportunities (buds) in a particular solution.

When brainstorming roses, think about what things might go well for you at the outreach. In other words, what will you be looking for as marks of a successful program? The roses you identify in this exercise can be used later for creating program outcomes.

The buds are areas of opportunity. What are some places where your outreach might be able to grow? Are there partners who may want to connect with you after you have a successful outreach event? Will doing a pilot program open up a door to receiving grant funding?

Thorns are unpleasant surprises. Brainstorm what might go wrong. By thinking about possible downsides and likely difficulties before the outreach, you can plan for surprises before they occur. Every technology-based outreach can write down technology failure as a thorn. Identifying such problems early on means you'll have a backup plan for when the Wi-Fi goes down or a computer breaks. When your team plans for thorns early in the process, everyone will feel prepared to get right back on track instead of feeling panicked.

Perform this exercise before you move into a pilot program. Give yourself an opportunity to plan for the unknown, prepare for exploring new opportunities that may appear, and keep an eye out for potential successes. You can also use this exercise as an evaluation tool by doing it again after the pilot program has ended. When working through this exercise as an evaluator, ask these questions: "What was a success?" "What opportunities presented themselves?" and "What challenges did we face?" Used after a program this exercise becomes a fantastic reflection tool!

❯ ROSE, THORN, BUD

SUPPLIES

> Three different colors of sticky notes
> Markers
> Whiteboard or large sheet of paper

SETUP

1. Hand out sticky notes and markers. Be sure to give everyone a few sticky notes of each color.
2. Choose one solution to start. You can repeat this exercise with many different solutions before moving into prototyping and piloting.
3. Place a sticky note from each color on the board, writing on each whether it represents a rose, thorn, or bud.
4. Write the solution on the board.

STEPS

1. Explain that this exercise looks at potential successes (roses), threats (thorns), and opportunities (buds).
2. Choose a different color for roses, thorns, and buds.
3. Give the team five to seven minutes to brainstorm as many roses, thorns, and buds as possible, noting that each person should identify at least one from each group. Have team members write their ideas on the corresponding colored sticky notes and then place them on the board.
4. At the end of the time, discuss all the ideas with the team, grouping them into similar categories or themes. Ask, "Are any of the roses, thorns, or buds connected to one another?" Draw the relationships that the team members note by circling and labeling themes, with lines bridging interconnected ideas.
5. Discuss what you as a team might do to prepare yourselves for this outreach moving forward. Identify any major stumbling blocks that make this particular solution infeasible.
6. Repeat this exercise with different solutions.

HOW CAN YOU TRY OUT SOLUTIONS TO YOUR PROBLEM?

Prototyping is a safe way for you to quickly and inexpensively try out your project idea with staff and/or stakeholders before jumping into the real thing. Use prototypes to explore what may work and what may need to be changed. You can fail quickly, iterate, and evaluate as many times as you feel necessary before being comfortable enough with the solution to move into the pilot program stage. These exercises bring to the surface what tools you

Don't be afraid to try out different prototyping exercises with the same solution. Each of these exercises brings to the surface unique aspects of the program design. Break teams into smaller groups to prototype the same solution. Different groups of people will often come up with vastly different program ideas based on the same solution.

might need, where you may run into issues, the steps you need to take to run the program, and much more.

❯ RAPID PROTOTYPING

Rapid prototyping involves building a representation of your final outreach solution; you will manipulate ideas quickly and iterate efficiently. This is the perfect opportunity to use the supplies in the design thinking kit you built early on in this process (see chapter 5). Find assorted office supplies or other odds and ends you have around the office to give team members a fun selection of materials to use in building their prototypes. The supply list provided here gives just some possible examples of materials to include.

SUPPLIES

> Colored paper
> Markers
> Tape
> Glue
> Aluminum foil
> Clay
> Pipe cleaners
> LEGOs
> Felt
> Magazines

SETUP

1. Arrange supplies in the room so that they are accessible to all.
2. Separate the team into groups of three to four people. If this is the size of your whole team, then work as one group.
3. Keep in mind that prototyping can be noisy. Ensure that each team has enough space to work without disrupting other teams. Some teams may need to leave the main meeting room while they build their prototypes.

STEPS

1. Have each team pick a solution to prototype, or have everyone prototype the same solution. It can be fun to see how varied

the ideas are for a solution prototype when everyone is working toward the same end goal. Oftentimes, the best final product comes from the intersection of these prototypes.

2. Give teams fifteen minutes to design a prototype using the provided supplies. Prototypes may be a physical manifestation of an object, a drawing of a website, or a mockup of a service, to give just a few examples. There are no right or wrong approaches!

3. At the end of the fifteen minutes, have each team explain its prototype to the larger group, which should give feedback. Remember to build off of ideas; don't shut them down. Think, "Yes, and . . ." instead of "No, but . . ."

4. After all teams have received feedback, give them a chance to iterate. Explain that they can build something new from scratch or alter their first versions. Give ten minutes for iteration.

5. Then, have the teams share their revisions, explaining how they have improved their prototypes. At this stage, ask teams to discuss how they might take their ideas from the prototype stage into a real-world pilot program. What resources would they need to make that happen?

6. Depending on the nature of the prototypes, your team may choose to invite stakeholders to build and/or interact with their designs. Getting feedback this early in the design process helps to identify more nuanced needs that can be addressed in the pilot program.

7. Discuss the findings as a group. Assign a note taker to record key points about supplies needed, people to contact, lesson plans, and so forth—anything that might be needed to move the rapid prototype into a pilot outreach program.

❯ ACT IT OUT

Getting up on our feet and acting out a solution shows us how it would work in the real world. We can step into the shoes of our stakeholders, anticipating their interactions with our outreach. Just as we are all artists in design thinking, so too are we all actors. Performing short skits gets our brains thinking about a solution in a different way than does seeing it in a model or drawn on paper.

SUPPLIES

> › Space to perform

SETUP

1. Separate your team into groups of three to four people. If this is the size of your whole team, then work as one group.
2. Keep in mind that rehearsing for this prototype can be noisy. Ensure that each team has enough space to work without disrupting other teams. Some teams may need to leave the main meeting room while they plan their prototypes.

STEPS

1. Pick a unique solution for each group to act out or have everyone act out the same solution.
2. Give teams fifteen minutes to plan their skits, which should last from two to four minutes. Explain that every member of each team should have a part. Note that skits can take any format, for example, play, song, or commercial—there are no limits.
3. At the end of the fifteen minutes, have all groups perform their skits, one at a time.
4. After each skit, ask questions and give feedback.
5. When all skits are completed, discuss them as a group. Assign a note taker to record key points about supplies needed, people to contact, lesson plans, and so forth. Record anything that might be needed in order to move the prototyped skit into a pilot outreach program.

❯ COVER STORY MOCKUP

A cover story mockup explores the details of a program from a different perspective than is typically used in prototyping. Teams pretend as if the outreach has already happened and a magazine has chosen to write a story about its success. What would a journalist write about your outreach? Through this exercise, you will brainstorm completed outreach activities, including what outcomes were measured, what challenges you faced, and so on.

SUPPLIES

> 11-×-17-inch sheets of paper
> Markers
> Scissors
> Tape

SETUP

1. Arrange supplies in the room so that they are accessible to all. Each team will need at least one sheet of paper and markers. The paper will be folded to resemble a magazine. Extra sheets of paper may be used to create the internal content.
2. Separate the team into groups of three to four people. If this is the size of your whole team, then work as one group.
3. Keep in mind that this prototyping exercise can be noisy. Ensure that each team has enough space to work without disrupting other teams. Some teams may need to leave the main meeting room while they create their mockups.

STEPS

1. Direct each team to create a magazine article about the outreach program your library is designing. Explain that they should imagine that the program has already been completed. Have each team choose an appropriate real-world magazine and then draw its masthead on the front page, add a cover image, and write a title to the story.

> **Storyboarding is another fun way to prototype.** See the instructions for that exercise earlier in this chapter's section on brainstorming solutions.

2. Direct teams to fill the inside of their magazines with stats, quotes, photos, and the first paragraph of their articles. Ask, "What outcomes would a journalist want to write about?" and "What would the public want to know about your outreach?"
3. Give each team twenty minutes to complete this exercise.
4. After the twenty minutes, come back together as a group to share the magazines.

5. Discuss the magazines as a group. Assign a note taker to record key points about supplies needed, people to contact, lesson plans, and so forth. Record anything that might be needed in order to move a magazine outreach idea into a pilot outreach program.

6. Hold on to these magazines; they are effective tools to use when presenting your outreach to stakeholders and administration.

HOW DO YOU TURN PROTOTYPES INTO REAL-WORLD OUTREACH PROGRAMS?

In this next stage, your team will take a prototyped solution and turn it into actual outreach that serves the public. However, this is not yet a full commitment. You are not agreeing to do outreach at a location every week for a year. Instead, you will be launching a pilot program.

Pilots are short runs of a program that are executed while your design is mostly finished. Instead of waiting until you reach 100 percent completion, with a pilot you can move forward with only 80 percent of the planning finished. You want to run a pilot before all the program details are ironed out to give yourself room for failure and opportunities for iteration and improvement. You won't yet be locked in to a large financial or time commitment. You will have the space and time to change the details as you learn.

Piloting Outreach Programs

The piloting stage is not the time to commit all your resources. Look at the different solutions your team prototyped. Choose one solution that your team thinks best solves your problem. Identify the key components you will need to make the outreach happen. Oftentimes, pilots are scaled-back versions of the final product. Perhaps the final outreach will have ten computer stations and five staff members, while the pilot may have only two computers and one staff member. Focus on the key elements that solve your problem; don't get lost in the details.

To operate a successful pilot, you will need to consider several different questions:

1. Where will you get the money to run the pilot?

2. How will you advertise the pilot?

3. What talking points will staff use when discussing the outreach with the public? These can also be used as entry points for collecting user feedback. For example: "This is a pilot program we're running. We are doing this to see what works and what doesn't before we invest more time and money. Can you help us improve by answering a couple of questions?"
4. How are you going to assess what is working? Decide what metrics you will want to use to evaluate the pilot.
5. What outcomes do you need to see in order to move from the pilot phase into implementing the full project?
6. How will you collect feedback from patrons? Some options include surveys and comment cards.
7. How will you provide evidence of what occurred during the outreach? Consider taking photos to reflect upon after the program.

After each pilot run, come together with staff to discuss what happened. Be okay with failure. Now is the time to discover that something is not working so you can go back to the drawing board with the team. Some questions to consider include these:

> › What went wrong?
> › Is the technology still applicable but the audience is wrong?
> › Was it the wrong location?
> › How can you design a new prototype and do another pilot run?

If needed, return to the list of brainstormed solutions and choose a new idea. Everything you learn in this pilot stage will help to inform other possible solutions.

HOW DO YOU KNOW IF THE OUTREACH IS WORKING?

Evaluation is a critical piece of any project. From the very beginning of your outreach planning you have to ask, "What problem are we trying to solve?" The answer to this question comes from the work your team did in the earlier Problem Statement—Asking "How might we . . . ?" exercise. When you understand the problem you are trying to solve, you can develop programs with a clear understanding of what you are trying to achieve. To see if your work is solving a problem and meeting those goals, you have to evaluate.

Traditionally, libraries have evaluated only the inputs and outputs of their programming. Although these are important parts of evaluating a program, they do not show the whole picture. Instead, you have to focus your attention on measuring outcomes. Outcomes, defined as benefits to people, indicate when positive changes have occurred in participants based on their library use. These positive changes occur in participants' "skill, knowledge, attitude, behavior, condition, or life status."[3] By measuring outcomes, you will be able to hear the voices of the participants and pull out that human experience, something that cannot be told through inputs and outputs alone.[4] Figure 6.2 shows a sample tracking worksheet for outcomes.

Having an evaluation plan is critical to the success of future planning. You have to be able to tell a story by understanding what happened, what impact you made, and how people's lives were improved by interacting with library services. Stories about project outcomes can be shared at city council meetings and with library boards and administrators to impress upon them the value of the services the library provides. Meaningful evaluations paint a

Expected Outputs	Actual Outputs	Target Met?	Expected Outcomes	Actual Outcomes	Target Met?
100 participants	112	Yes	75% report increase in confidence online	90% increase confidence	Yes
12 job training classes	5 job training classes	No	5 participants secured a new job	1 new job secured	No
1,000 hours laptop usage	1,210	Yes	50% brought in a new person to outreach	30% brought in a new person	No
3 laundromat partners	2 partners	No			
60 laptops purchased and used	60 laptops purchased and used	Yes			

FIGURE 6.2 Outcomes Tracking Worksheet

> **Inputs are the internal resources that go into the creation of a program.** These resources include such things as the money spent, the number of staff involved, and the time staff spent on the program. Outputs are the measurable products of a program. Relevant data might include the number of people who attended a program, how many hours people spent reading, or the number of books checked out.

picture for you and your staff and give you quantifiable metrics that you can use to improve your outreach.

Deciding What to Evaluate

It is tempting to measure the success of any program, inside or outside the library, by the number of people who attended. However, that data point tells you next to nothing and should never be the sole metric used in evaluating the success of a program. For example, many people in attendance at your outreach event or program may indicate that the subject matter was appealing or that your marketing campaign was successful, but it's also possible that the day was hot and many people were simply looking for something to do where air conditioning was available. Just knowing how many people attended does not give you any information about whether you solved your problem or had any impact on patrons' lives. Expanding your evaluation to include outcomes gives you clear goals for improving future services.

You already have the framework in place to be successful in evaluating your outreach. Through the human-centered design thinking exercises in this book, you have learned how to speak with your community members to assess their needs and how to define the problem you are trying to solve. The next step is to brainstorm indicators to look for during an outreach to see if your goals are being met. Ask, "What change in skill, knowledge, attitude, behavior, condition, or life status do we want people to have when they leave our outreach?"

Although every outreach will be different, here are some core indicators you can tweak to meet your specific needs:

> Did the users' knowledge increase?
> Was confidence gained?

> Were people collaborating?
> What skills were learned?
> Will users behave differently after the outreach?

Logic Models

To develop outcomes, I recommend using a basic logic model. Logic models are "a systematic and visual way to present and share your understanding of the relationships among the resources you have to operate your program, the activities you plan, and the changes or results you hope to achieve."[5] You can utilize a logic model to tell the story of your outreach and what changes will occur in participants. The model then becomes an engaging and effective tool to use with stakeholders, both internal and external, to show how their involvement in the project creates impact. Figure 6.3 shows a sample logic model template provided by the University of Wisconsin–Extension. This and other templates for download and additional resources are available through UW Extension at https://fyi.uwex.edu/programdevelopment/logic-models.

The logic model, like all other tools used in design thinking, is flexible; return to it throughout the life of a project. As time progresses, you might find that pieces need to be updated. You can "get meta" here and evaluate your evaluation methods. Nothing in your entire design thinking process is static. You should feel free to revisit tools at any stage during your planning or even after the outreach has launched. By having a continuous evaluation cycle, you are free to iterate regularly.

To build your logic model, you will need to think about five different metrics: resources, activities, outputs, outcomes, and impacts. The model displays these visually in order to read it from left to right using "If . . . , then . . ." statements to connect all the different parts. Through the model, you are setting clear expectations about how and why your outreach will operate.

The first section of the model is your planned work, what you need to do to get your outreach up and running:

> Resources are the human, financial, organizational, and community assets that you have available to direct toward your outreach.
> Activities are what you do with those resources. They might be processes, techniques, tools, events, technology, and/or actions taken.

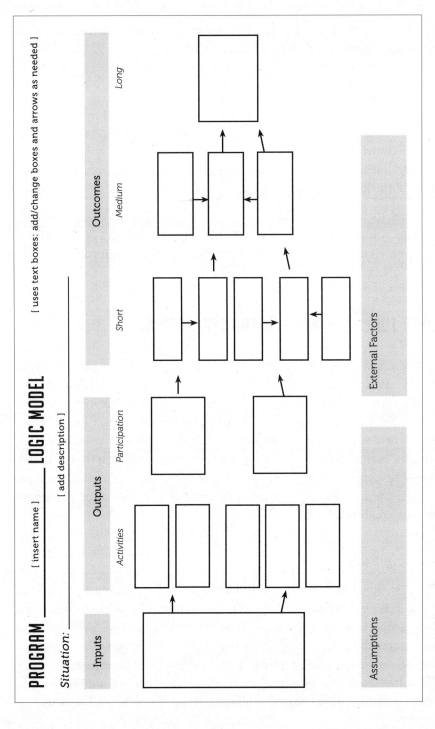

FIGURE 6.3 Logic Model Worksheet Source: University of Wisconsin–Extension, https://fyi.uwex.edu/programdevelopment/logic-models.

The next section of the model is about the outreach's intended results. What is going to happen because of your outreach?

> Outputs are the direct results of the outreach. These have a quantitative value.
> Outcomes measure the specific changes in outreach participants' behavior, knowledge, skills, status, and/or level of functioning. These are short-term changes.
> Impacts include the fundamental changes in participants in the long term, say, seven to ten years out.

Although logic models can help you to brainstorm what to measure and what changes you want to see occurring in participants, they don't tell you how to gain such data. To do that, you will need to connect with participants by building surveys and other evaluation tools.

WHAT TOOLS CAN YOU USE FOR EVALUATION?

Evaluation can be tricky for libraries. We often get only one opportunity to interact with the people who participate in our programs. Measuring long-term changes, in particular, may be nigh on impossible for one-time programs, but for recurring events, we can plan for the impact we want and do our best to measure that impact whenever we can. Our traditional, output-only evaluation models don't give us enough information to truly understand the impact of our work. There are tools, however, that will enable us to measure the impact of our work, allowing us to iterate or end programs based on real-world data.

Writing Surveys

The first skill you will need to develop is writing a decent survey. Robust surveys give you quality data. Don't fall into the trap of writing surveys that drive people to answer positively. You cannot gather critical feedback about your outreach programming if you ask only how much someone enjoyed it. Instead, surveys should be driven by the outcomes you are trying to achieve. Think back to the problem you are trying to solve and the aspirations your team brainstormed at the very beginning of the project. How will you know if you are meeting those goals? Frame questions that will assist you in determining whether you are solving your problem. Figure 6.4 provides a sample survey.

Before you even get into writing questions, talk with your team about how you will be delivering the survey to patrons. Will it be online, in person, or over the phone? Will staff ask questions directly or will participants fill out a form on their own? Will this be a survey for staff to fill out after an outreach, for participants to do during the event, or for attendees to complete at home as a follow-up survey? Regardless of the format of the survey, you will need to follow some best practices:

> **Include instructions.** Explain to participants why the survey is important and, if necessary, how they are supposed to answer the questions.

> **Create short surveys.** Participants are unlikely to complete surveys that last for many pages. This is especially true if your library uses surveys regularly during outreach programming. Think short, sweet, and to the point. Ask only those questions that will get you valuable answers that you can use in evaluation.

> **Write simple questions.** Avoid using library jargon and abbreviations.

> **Write for all users' reading levels.** Writing overly complicated questions may prevent users with lower reading levels or English language learners from participating in surveys. Know your audience. Utilize tools such as ReadablePro (https://readable.io/text) to test out text reading levels and adjust your writing as needed.

> **Ask one thing at a time.** In order to effectively read the data you collect, ask only one thing in each question. When you solicit multiple answers in one question, interpreting what exactly a person is responding to can be challenging.

> **Avoid leading or biased questions.** This can be a tricky one! The most common leading questions are formatted like this: "Why did you enjoy this outreach?" Asking this type of

DATA EQUITY FOR MAIN STREET
PARTICIPANT EVALUATION

These questions are used to help improve our curriculum, not to test you. Thank you for your feedback!

Class 1	
After this class, do you feel like you have a better understanding of what open data is?	Y \ N
How would you define open data?	
After this class, do you feel like you have a better understanding of how open data is used?	Y \ N
Do you have a personal question that you think you can answer with open data?	Y \ N
What is your question?	
How likely are you to attend the next class?	Very / Somewhat / Not Very
If you are likely to attend the next class, what do you most want to learn? If you are not likely to take the next class, why not?	
We love feedback. Do you have any additional feedback about the curriculum or instruction?	

FIGURE 6.4 **Program Survey from Data Equity for Main Street**

question assumes the user had a positive experience and will
result in positive feedback.

> **Create a logical flow to the order of questions.** Ask the
  easiest questions first, building up to questions that require
  longer responses. Arrange questions to follow the flow of
  the outreach, structuring the survey so that questions align
  with what happened at the beginning, middle, and end of the
  outreach.

> **Maintain privacy.** Very rarely will you require a patron's
  personally identifiable information for a survey. If for some
  reason you do require it, remember to follow proper informed
  consent guidelines.[6]

Surveying participants is not the only way to evaluate your outreach. Patrons
will quickly get burned out from answering too many surveys. No one wants
to be asked a barrage of questions every time he or she interacts with the
library. Instead, consider adding staff surveys to the mix. Facilitator surveys
give staff the opportunity to reflect on their work, to note whether the indicators they were looking for during the outreach show whether the desired
outcomes have been reached. Craft the facilitator surveys using the same
best practices as are used for participants. However, feel free to use library
terminology, increase the reading level, and ask more complex questions as
appropriate. Try to keep a healthy balance between staff and patron surveys
so as not to overburden either group with answering questions.

>>>

In addition to surveys, consider other ways you can gather information
about whether your targets are being met. Taking photos during an outreach
is a great way to capture learning outcomes. Photos give you an opportunity to reflect on an event and tell a visual story. Another tool is a comment
card with a single question. Consider asking a different question each time
to gather feedback that will demonstrate if you are meeting your preestablished outcomes. In Wisconsin, Madison Public Library's Teen Bubbler program uses cards designed to look like a phone (see figure 6.5). Participants
can use the cards to leave short feedback that gives you a quick snapshot of

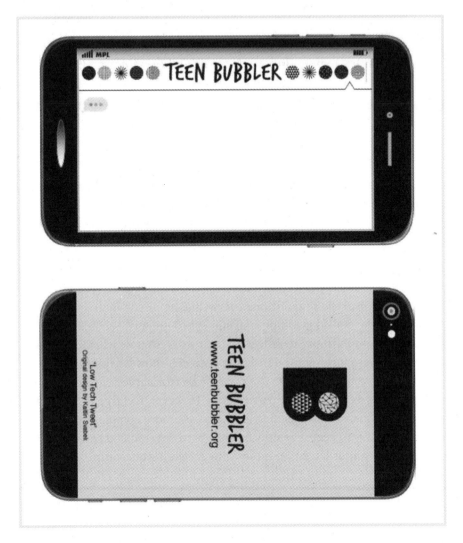

**FIGURE 6.5 Low-Tech Tweet Participant Feedback Card
(Front and Back)**

Source: Madison (WI) Public Library's Teen Bubbler Program; design by Kaitlin Svabek.

their program experience. Although not nearly as robust as surveys, comment cards do capture data about how well an outreach program is working. They also are wonderful marketing tools to communicate with stakeholders about the impact of your work through the words of participants.

The method you use to evaluate is less important than the evaluation itself. Whatever tools you choose to use, make sure you are putting the thought needed into measuring the outcomes of your work. Design thinking is an iterative process. Once you have evaluated your efforts, go back to the exercises listed earlier in this chapter, brainstorm other ways of achieving your goals, and tweak your outreach plans as needed.

NOTES

1. Rikke Dam and Teo Siang, "Stage 2 in the Design Thinking Process: Define the Problem and Interpret the Results," The Interaction Design Foundation, posted August 2017, www.interaction-design.org/literature/article/stage-2-in -the-design-thinking-process-define-the-problem-and-interpret-the-results.
2. "Turning Outward Resources for Libraries," American Library Association, "Tools, Publications, and Resources," August 1, 2017, www.ala.org/tools/librariestransform/ libraries-transforming-communities/resources-for-library -professionals.
3. "Outcome Based Evaluation Basics," Institute of Museum and Library Services, accessed June 18, 2018, www.imls.gov/grants/outcome-based -evaluation/basics.
4. Melissa Gross, Cindy Mediavilla, and Virginia A. Walter, *Five Steps of Outcome-Based Planning and Evaluation for Public Libraries* (Chicago: ALA Editions, 2016).
5. W.K. Kellogg Foundation, *W.K. Kellogg Foundation Logic Model Development Guide* (Battle Creek, MI: W.K. Kellogg Foundation, January 2004), 17. Available as a PDF from www.wkkf.org/resource-directory/resource/2006/02/wk-kellogg-foundation -logic-model-development-guide.
6. Project Outcome (Measuring the True Impact of Public Libraries), "Writing Open-Ended Survey Questions," accessed July 3, 2018, www.projectoutcome.org/ surveys-resources/writing-open-ended-questions.

PLANNING TECHNOLOGY-
BASED OUTREACH

A Design Thinking Journey
from Start to Finish

Moving from problem to solution can sometimes feel like a daunting task. The exercises provided in the previous chapter of this book provide a road map for success. Working through each of the exercises teaches you new skills that can be adapted for any project you may be working on at your library. As you learn each of the exercises in this book (and discover new ones from other resources), you will gain the ability to determine which ones fit each specific project's needs. At times you may follow chapter 6's guide from start to finish, in its entirety. Other times you may find that just one or two steps are enough to spark innovative problem solving. Design thinking exercises are structured to help your staff work smarter, not harder; to think outside the box; and to keep the user front and center.

After seeing only the instructions for each exercise, as presented in chapter 6, you may find yourself scratching your head, wondering how in the world to apply those exercises to a real-world technology-based outreach problem. This chapter demonstrates one journey following chapter 6's road map. In this chapter, you will read about a sample project in which a small team worked through each of the exercises presented in this book to go from a broad idea about doing technology-based outreach all the way through to a prototype. I will walk you through our team's process, explaining how and why different decisions were made, showing how each exercise builds upon the last, and providing real-world applications for these tools that you can use to create stellar outreach programs at your library.

WHAT ARE OUR ASPIRATIONS AND BARRIERS?

We all have hopes and dreams for the services we provide to our communities. Taking time to talk about them with the project team is usually the first step I take when we begin our design process.

Setting aside a dedicated time to list the aspirations we have for a new service model allows staff to share their personal outlooks for the future of our project. When our team comes together for this initial kick-off meeting, I often hear new ideas that had not occurred to me before. Together, we discuss what our goals are, sussing out the details that will help us move forward into defining the problem we want to solve.

When beginning this sample project, we started with nothing more than the idea that our library wanted to start doing technology-based outreach in our community. Many of you may be starting with this same basic premise for your outreach. We identified a desire for this new service model and began talking about what our aspirations were for future technology-based outreach programming. Everyone on the team was given a package of sticky notes and a Sharpie and encouraged to write down or draw their aspirations. As an idea was developed, each person put it on the whiteboard, calling out the aspiration to the team as it was placed. Announcing aspirations allows other team members to quickly build upon one another's ideas.

We performed this exercise quickly, allowing time after aspirations were generated to process and group them into categories based on similar

Be sure to define the aspirations that you have for your technology-based outreach program. Do you hope that seniors will feel more comfortable checking out e-books from the library? Do you want the library to provide technology equity for the community, ensuring all residents have access? Or do you want to increase your local teens' ability to creatively solve problems? Knowing where you're headed will help ensure success.

themes (see figure 7.1). Our team brainstormed aspirations for technology-based outreach programming that could achieve the following:

> Reduce fear
> Teach creative problem solving
> Create opportunity for learning
> Increase curiosity
> Build/create a tech-comfy community
> Level the playing field
> Increase skills
> Boost socioeconomic status
> Reach nonusers
> Introduce new technology and opportunities for practice

Once our aspirations were identified, we had to flip our perspective: What barriers might we face that would prevent us from achieving the goals we just outlined? None of us like thinking about what might go wrong. However, when we are able to identify those challenges from the start, we have an opportunity to plan and not be surprised when they occur. Having a list of potential barriers can also help us when we move on to identifying the problem we want to solve. A barrier might be an indicator as to where we

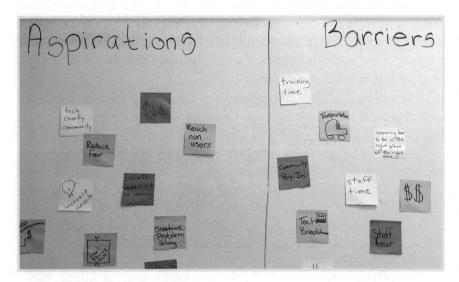

FIGURE 7.1 **Aspirations and Barriers**

should focus our technology-based outreach. Barriers can help us to focus our attention and narrow the scope of our new service.

Using the same techniques as when we brainstormed our aspirations, our team began writing down all the barriers we might face in launching technology-based outreach programming in our community:

> › Funding
> › Staff fears
> › Knowing how to be in the right place at the right time
> › Time
> › Community buy-in
> › Apathy
> › Transportation
> › Training time
> › Library being seen as more than books
> › Technology failures/breakdown

WHAT PROBLEM ARE WE TRYING TO SOLVE?

Identifying all the hopes, dreams, fears, and challenges for our technology-based outreach unified our team. Everyone began feeling excited and ready to tackle one of the most challenging parts of the design thinking process: defining the problem we wanted to solve. One of the most intimidating parts of this exercise is knowing that the question the team develops will lead the rest of the design process.

Something that helps calm my nerves when moving into this stage of the design process is remembering that nothing is ever written in stone. Design thinking gives us the flexibility to return to previous stages of our work and reassess based on new learning. All our projects are continually growing and changing.

Although it is true that your team should be thoughtful and dedicate enough time to writing your problem statement, you should never feel trapped by it. The problem statement should be a healthy, inspiring challenge for your team to meet head-on.

You might have program details in mind when you begin this process, but you may quickly discover your plan doesn't meet your community's needs in the way you thought it would. Come into the process being flexible, with an open mind, and it is likely you will find a new depth to your original idea (or change it entirely).

Problem statements need to be broad in scope so there are lots of different solutions. The solution should never be part of the statement. This approach narrows down our options to developing only one solution.

I like to begin this exercise by giving each person some sticky notes and markers. Everyone on the team took five minutes to write down their problem statements (everything after the "How might we . . ."). As each idea was generated, the team member said the statement out loud and placed it on the board (see figure 7.2).

Because we were working with a small group for this sample project, we refined ideas together as we developed them. One person wrote the top ideas on the whiteboard, which gave us the opportunity to talk about them in more depth and edit them as we saw fit. We performed this exercise

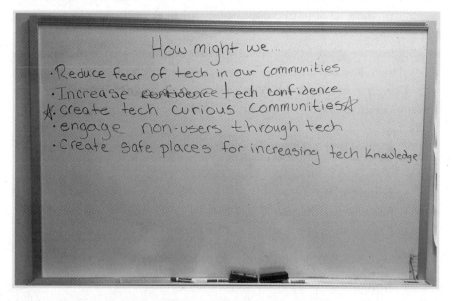

FIGURE 7.2 **Problem Statements—Asking "How might we . . . ?"**

immediately after finishing the Aspirations and Barriers exercise. The board with those brainstormed ideas was still hanging in the room for all of us to see. Looking at the following potential "How might we . . . ?" problem statements, you can see the influence the first exercise had on the second; our statements were built right out of the aspirations and barriers we had identified. "How might we . . ."

> reduce fear of technology in our communities?
> increase technology confidence?
> create technology-curious communities?
> engage nonusers through technology?
> create safe places for increasing technical knowledge?

WHO ARE OUR STAKEHOLDERS?

Far too often we get tunnel vision when it comes to our library services. We consider only the stakeholders who will be the direct beneficiaries of our work. It is easy to forget the rest of the people who are impacted in some way by our new service or program. Identifying all our stakeholders, and the level to which they will be impacted by our technology-based outreach, will show us potential opportunity areas or obstacles we may need to overcome.

Because we started this project with no more knowledge than that we wanted to do a technology-based outreach of some kind, we had to come up with a core group of stakeholders first. Once we had determined our core stakeholder groups, we built our circle of influence from the middle out (see figure 7.3).

We decided to put three different user groups into our core stakeholder ring:

> Library staff
> School-aged children
> Caregivers (parents and guardians)

In the direct stakeholder ring we placed these groups:

> Nonusers
> Teachers

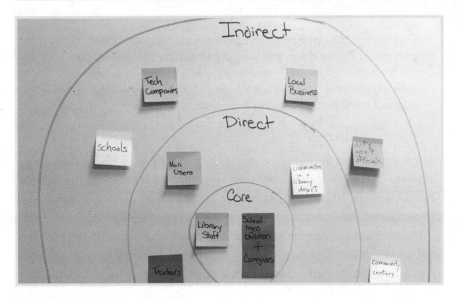

FIGURE 7.3 **Stakeholder Map**

> Outreach site hosts
> Communities in a library district

Last, we identified our indirect stakeholders:

> Technology companies
> Local businesses
> City government officials
> Community centers
> Schools

HOW CAN WE GAIN INSIGHTS FROM OUR STAKEHOLDERS?

We had now established a problem statement—"How might we create technology-curious communities?"—and several different layers of potential stakeholders on which to focus our solutions. Before getting started on brainstorming possible solutions to our problem statement, we needed to gather more information about our stakeholders. This is typically referred to as the gaining insights phase of a design thinking project. In this stage,

> **You can gather information about your stakeholder groups in many different ways.** The How Do You Gain Insights from Stakeholders? section in chapter 6 provides a variety of options for connecting with stakeholders. Each conversation or survey will give you new insights into the best possible way to serve your community.

we wanted to find at least one way of connecting with our stakeholders. Remember, this is a human-centered process; we are designing for people. This requires us to connect with them directly, not just forge ahead with design based on our own assumptions or expert knowledge.

For this sample project we decided to focus on the Interviews exercise. Looking at our stakeholder groups, we started brainstorming more specifics about whom we wanted to interview:

> Teachers
> School administrators
> After-school staff
> Parents/caregivers
> Community program leaders
> Library media specialists
> Library staff
> Technology experts
> Students in third through seventh grades
> High school students

After looking at whom we would interview, we thought about potential places we could reach these stakeholders to conduct one-on-one interviews:

> Community centers
> Library
> Businesses

> **You might not** connect with every group or visit all of the locations you brainstorm, but it is a good idea to come up with lots of ideas first and then begin to narrow down your choices based on your needs and resources.

> Schools (elementary, middle, high)
> After-school facilities

Looking at our long lists of stakeholders and locations, we began to think about the practical aspects of interviewing. Who were the most important people to speak with? Which stakeholders would provide the most insights into creating solutions to our problem? We narrowed down our interviewee list to these stakeholder groups:

> Third, sixth, and eighth grade students
> Parents/caregivers
> Library staff
> Teachers

We then assigned two staff members to each stakeholder group. Team members determined locations they felt were best for conducting the interviews. Our group then spent time brainstorming interview questions we could ask our different stakeholder groups (see figure 7.4). The questions we developed were mostly around technology but also tried to focus on people's core desires and beliefs. Some of these questions would be asked of every stakeholder group while others were directed toward a selected few:

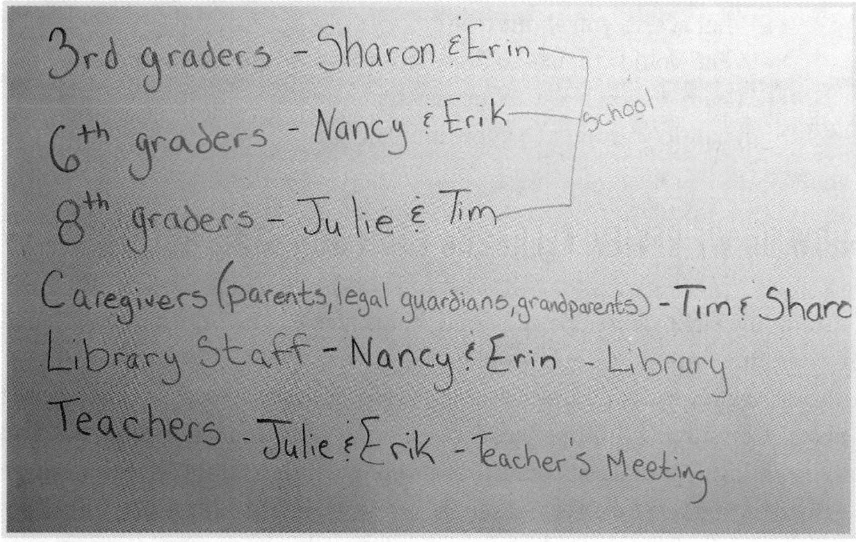

FIGURE 7.4 **Interview Planning**

> You can learn a lot from asking more broad questions. If you focus only on technology, you might miss out on a novel idea that is sparked by a question about creativity or what someone is interested in learning.

> Where do you use technology?
> What kinds of technology do you use?
> Is there technology you use only with others?
>> What is it and how do you use it?
> What is your favorite technology and why?
>> What is your favorite technology to use at work?
> In what ways do you see technology making your life easier? Harder?
> Are there technology limits in your home?
> Do you have self-imposed technology limits?
> In what ways do you use technology as a family?
> What are you curious about?
> How is technology used in your classroom?
> What is your dream scenario for using technology in the classroom?
> What scares you about technology?
> What would you like to do with technology but don't know how?
> Where do you learn about new technology?
> What do you want to know more about?

HOW DO WE REVIEW FEEDBACK FROM OUR STAKEHOLDERS?

Asking the right questions of people helps give us the information needed to design solutions to our problem. However, we have to be able to process all the information that we receive during the previous gaining insights phase. Conducting multiple sessions or types of insight collection will lead to amassing a lot of data! We have to be able to interrupt the information we gained during these exercises to make our work worthwhile. Time for reflection and analysis enables identification of themes across groups, guiding the team toward a solution that meets the needs of all stakeholders.

We began to digest our findings by having a team meeting during which we discussed our interviews in an open format. Feedback that stood out or comments we heard repeatedly were written on sticky notes and placed on the wall where everyone could refer to them throughout the meeting. Having an open, safe discussion about the data we gathered during interviews is where we like to start. Sharing insights within the group helps to get everyone on the same page before moving forward.

One of the things I love most about design thinking is having a toolkit filled with exercises that I can utilize to process information. The rules of brainstorming (see chapter 5) along with a variety of different exercises (see chapter 6) provide a framework for generating ideas quickly with a group of people. It can be challenging to take a pile of data gathered from interview sessions and know how to best understand what people are thinking, feeling, or doing. Team discussions are a great first step in processing the information learned during the gaining insights exercises. We start off broad and then dive in deep. My favorite tool for deep dives is an empathy map.

Empathy maps are a fairly simple tool that we use to gain a deeper insight into what our stakeholders are thinking and feeling, saying and doing, hearing and seeing. Instead of looking at individuals, the team builds user personas to analyze the insights gained during interviews, focus groups, and/or design workshops.

Empathy maps are divided into six segments, with the stakeholder represented in the middle (see figure 7.5). We thought about all the interview data gathered from speaking with teachers and used that to create a representative persona of "the teacher." As ours was a small group, we decided to do the empathy map together by drawing it on the whiteboard, rather than working on separate maps individually or in small teams.

When interviewing the teachers, we asked them to tell us what their ideal technology classroom looked like, what they feared, and what they wanted to learn more about. We uncovered a lot of great information from these interviews that gave us insights into how they view their role in creating technology-curious communities. We learned the following about teachers:

> They feel a lack of support.
> They are curious but feel trapped by their curricula.
> Some want to know more, but some also think it is not their job to teach technology in the classroom.

> They have heard about other schools having more access to technology than they do at their schools.

> Some have been told by their bosses that there just isn't enough time to add more technology training.

> Many talked about not having enough time.

> Some shifted the responsibility of technology training to after-school programs.

> Others do their best to integrate technology into their classrooms but see a lack of resources.

> They see students and parents struggling with technology.

> They face many barriers to becoming technology literate.

> They have many pain points, including a lack of money, time, and interest as well as fear.

> Many see opportunities to gain skills through professional development.

> Many want guidance on how to integrate technology into their curricula.

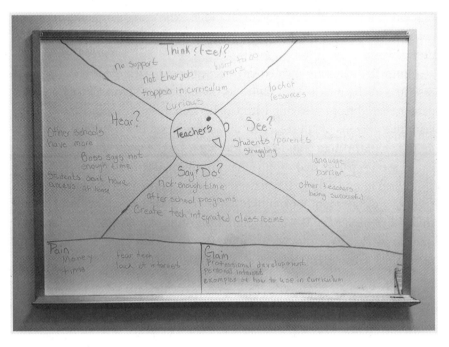

FIGURE 7.5 **Empathy Map**

HOW DO WE BRAINSTORM SOLUTIONS TO OUR PROBLEM?

A vibrant and dynamic portrait of our teachers was developed by creating our empathy map (see figure 7.5). Human-centered design is all about putting people front and center. We want to build programming based on our stakeholders' aspirations and needs, not our assumptions about them. Having a solid understanding of the people we are trying to reach informs all of our decisions as we move into brainstorming solutions.

Brainstorming solutions to our "How might we . . . ?" problem statement is usually thought of as the most fun part of the design process. In these exercises, everyone gets to flex their creative muscles, building upon the learning the team has discovered thus far. We often use multiple exercises in the brainstorming process as one informs the next, creating a rich set of ideas that can be pulled from to construct prototypes. Again, this is a process of starting big and broad, then narrowing down to flesh out a singular idea.

The first exercise that our team used to brainstorm solutions was Mind Maps. Mind maps start out with the "How might we . . . ?" question in the middle. Each branch from the middle becomes narrower until you get a specific solution to the problem. In our case, we started with five broad solution themes:

> Education
> Space
> Hardware
> Exploration
> Play

Each of these themes had branches of ideas that became more and more focused, drilling down to actual solutions. As we developed solutions, we continually referred back to our empathy map and the learning gained through speaking with stakeholders. Knowing that teachers expressed a desire for curriculum development, we drew a branch off of the education bubble on the mind map. We asked ourselves, "How could the library support curriculum development to create technology-curious communities?" Our team thought about developing curriculum suggestions and sharing them with schools or publishing curriculum ideas on our website. Each of these ideas was drawn as a branch, as we continued to build out the mind map.

Another solution to "How might we create technology-curious communities?" was doing outreach with hardware of some kind. From that broad idea, we thought about technology checkouts, computer labs to go, and technology device petting zoos. We further expanded on the technology checkout idea by using the information gained during our interviews, adding laptops, tablets, Wi-Fi, and e-readers to the map as branches off of the hardware bubble.

When our mind map was finished, we had many different starter ideas. The solutions brainstormed through a mind map are often in their infancy. They are the seeds of ideas that together provide a visual representation of solutions that can be expanded upon. Our mind map also laid out potential connections between different solutions. We saw that creating spaces where people could access technology was a valuable way to create technology-curious communities. This connected to our hardware solution, giving us the idea of creating a mobile computer lab or a technology-only library space in the community. The idea of combining spaces and hardware came up again in other brainstorming exercises and led us to creating a full prototype later on in our design process.

Building off of our mind map, we continued with another solution brainstorming exercise, the Creative Matrix (see figure 7.6). This is my favorite exercise because it generates a lot of solutions very quickly. In this exercise, everyone gets a chance to share their ideas, even if they find it challenging to contribute during the more vocal brainstorming sessions. Once again, each team member got a stack of sticky notes and a marker. We set the timer for ten minutes and everyone came up with at least one solution for each of the different intersections between stakeholder groups and service models.

For this exercise, we thought of three different service models for solving our problem: programs and services, partnerships, or technologies. Our team then brainstormed specific solutions for each of those categories as they aligned with a particular stakeholder group. We came up with the following potential solutions under programs and services:

> School-aged children
>> Techmobile
>> Technology petting zoo
>> Safety and privacy workshops
> Caregivers
>> Laundromat laptops
>> In-home iPad storytime training

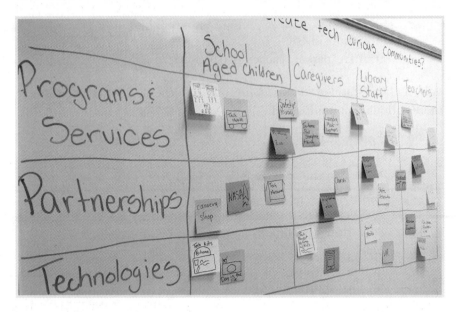

FIGURE 7.6 **Creative Matrix**

> Library staff
>> Train-the-trainer
>> Field trips to other libraries
> Teachers
>> Quick technology courses
>> Information literacy

When we looked at partnerships we came up with ideas:

> School-aged children
>> Camera shop
>> NASA (National Aeronautics and Space Administration)
>> Tech Museum
> Caregivers
>> Places of worship
>> Neighborhood associations
> Library staff
>> After-school care
>> State association
>> Technology companies

> Teachers
>> School district
>> PTA (parent-teacher association)

Last, we brainstormed solutions surrounding technologies that could create more curious communities:

> School-aged children
>> Technology kits at home
>> Day-in-the-life videos
> Caregivers
>> Technology projects to do at home
>> E-reader checkouts
> Library staff
>> Social media
>> Virtual reality
> Teachers
>> Recording equipment
>> Wearable technology
>> In-classroom play kits

Our creative matrix was now filled with more specific ideas for solving our problem.

HOW DO WE DECIDE WHICH SOLUTIONS TO PROTOTYPE?

To help us determine which solutions we wanted to explore in more depth, we used the Decision Matrix exercise as a guide to analyzing our solutions based on different metrics. Using ideas generated from our creative matrix, we looked at where each of the solutions fell in terms of cost and difficulty. Laying out our solutions on a decision matrix gave us a quick visual as to which ideas would be easy to implement right away and which ones would require greater investment to bring to fruition.

When analyzing our decision matrix (see figure 7.7), we discovered that some solutions, such as laundromat laptops and technology kits to take home, would be fairly simple for our staff to create but would take a lot of time and money to set up. On the other side of the spectrum, we saw that

Most libraries will find it is unrealistic to move every possible solution into the prototype stage of the design process. Large teams may come up with a lot of solutions to add to the matrix, some of them more far-fetched than others. You should always encourage wild ideas and outside-the-box thinking in your brainstorming sessions, but it is important to be thoughtful when choosing the solutions to move forward with in the design thinking process. Sometimes wild ideas may initially sound far-fetched but reveal upon further discussion bits and pieces that can be developed into a workable program.

it would be quite challenging to partner with NASA or the school districts on projects that would help us in creating technology-curious communities.

The decision matrix provided a great way for our team to visualize the solutions they wanted to explore in more depth through prototyping. To narrow down our list of solution options, we used the Rapid Voting exercise. Our team was able to quickly choose the solutions that seemed the most likely to solve our problem.

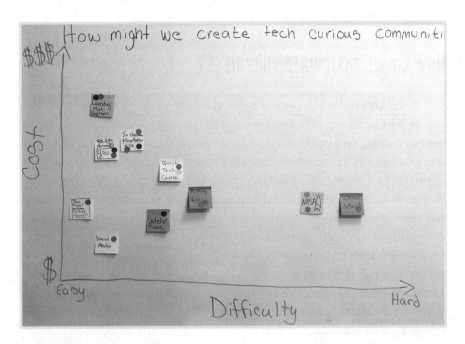

FIGURE 7.7 Decision Matrix

Rapid voting removes the "follow-the-leader" behavior exhibited in most team situations: team members often take on roles as leaders and followers; once a leader casts his or her vote for a solution, others are quick to follow suit. With rapid voting, everyone on the team uses stickers to indicate their votes at the same time, scrambling to the board together and placing their stickers as simultaneously as possible. This equals the playing field, giving a voice to those who might normally go unheard.

The three solutions we identified as the top choices to move forward into our prototyping stage were

> laundromat laptops,
> technology kits at home, and
> in-classroom play/explore kits.

Before we began prototyping these solutions, we used the Rose, Thorn, Bud exercise to examine the potential successes, challenges, and opportunities we might face when moving forward with implementing one of these solutions in the real world.

HOW DO WE ANTICIPATE SURPRISES?

The Rose, Thorn, Bud exercise is applicable at multiple points in the design process. I like to use it before prototyping so that we are cognizant of the rewards, risks, and opportunities as we move into shaping the details of implementation. The exercise can also be used as an evaluation tool, reflecting on the outreach after the fact. Either way, it is an important processing tool that gives us the insights needed to prepare us for piloting our outreach. No one likes to be surprised, caught off guard, or to miss opportunities when they present themselves. Through this exercise we identified all of these areas and prepared for them before dedicating a lot of staff time to the real-world solution.

Just because a solution is difficult doesn't mean it is not worth pursuing. You might choose to start with low-hanging fruit, but you can still map out a plan to achieve those more challenging projects in the future.

> **Keep all of** the artifacts your team creates during the design thinking exercises. Post them on the wall during team meetings to refer back to often. What you learned in one exercise will help guide you in the next.

We chose to use the laundromat laptop outreach for this exercise (see figure 7.8). We planned to repeat this exercise for all the solutions we chose to prototype. Each person on our team was given three sets of different-colored sticky notes to use as roses (successes), thorns (challenges), and buds (opportunities).

Our team identified many roses, thorns, and buds for a laundromat laptop outreach:

> Roses
>> An increase in computer skills
>> Employment opportunities
>> Third place
>> No wasted time
>> Increased curiosity
>> Building community
>> Less smelly people

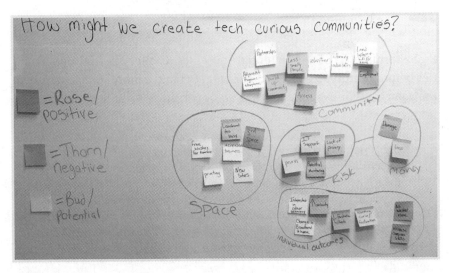

FIGURE 7.8   **Rose, Thorn, Bud**

> › Increased access
> › Less frustration with technology
- › Thorns
  - › Frustration overcoming the learning curve
  - › IT support
  - › Pornography
  - › Theft
  - › Laundromat too busy
  - › Parental monitoring
  - › Damage
  - › Lack of privacy
- › Buds
  - › Free washes for the homeless
  - › Partnerships
  - › New sites
  - › Adjacent programs (storytime, résumé building)
  - › Lending laptops and Wi-Fi at home
  - › Interest in other technology
  - › Increased business for laundromat
  - › Change in broadband usage at home
  - › Volunteers
  - › Library advocates
  - › Printing

Brainstorming all of the potential successes, challenges, and opportunities before prototyping allowed our team to build a more robust picture of the solution. For example, we saw an opportunity for free washes for the

Prototypes are an essential step in the design process allowing you to test out how a solution works before spending a lot of time and money on it. Think of prototyping as an outline of your project. A thoughtful prototype gives you a chance to see how the outreach will come together. By utilizing multiple prototyping exercises and/or having smaller groups prototype the same solutions, you can see different approaches to the same solution. Use the best parts of each prototype to design a great pilot project to test in your community.

homeless during the laptop lending outreach. We might have chosen to explore a solution wherein the laundromat donated washes to the homeless. This could have been partnered with an adjacent program such as résumé building. With clean clothing and a polished résumé, one outcome could have been an increase in employment among patrons at the outreach.

Another solution might have been to offer storytimes so that caregivers could learn computer skills while doing their laundry. This would have reduced the stress caretakers may feel when faced with having to find the time to do laundry, educate their children, and learn computer skills. With an increase in technology confidence, patrons might have wanted to check out a laptop and Wi-Fi hot spot to continue exploring when they were back at home (thereby creating a more technology-curious community).

HOW CAN WE TRY OUT SOLUTIONS TO OUR PROBLEM?

Solutions should always be investigated in more depth through prototyping exercises before devoting time and money to a full outreach or pilot. We regularly use four different prototyping exercises to take a quick look into the details of a potential program. Depending on the nature of the project, we may use only one of the exercises or we may use all of them. Our decision on which ones to use depends on the depth and breadth of the project. Each of the exercises draws out different focal points of a solution.

Storyboarding

Storyboarding is unique in that it can be used for brainstorming solutions, as presented in the Storyboards exercise in chapter 6, or as a prototyping tool. Either use of the tool is acceptable.

For our storyboard (see figure 7.9), we chose the solution of a laundromat laptop outreach. The drawings painted a picture of the outreach from start to finish. First, we secured our partner. Then, we wrote a supply list so that our IT department could purchase all the necessary equipment. Next, our team determined any furniture or other supplies that needed to be purchased. We scheduled dates with our partner, choosing times that we thought worked well for the community. Our staff then made plans for each

> **Explore what works** best for your team and the problem you are trying to solve. As you develop the storyboard, identify the processes you need to go through, challenges you may face, and opportunities to take advantage of when it comes to piloting your technology-based outreach.

of the visits and decided which outcomes to measure. We considered how the equipment and staff could arrive at the site. Last, we drew and discussed the outreach itself and patron feedback.

A storyboard is not a detailed plan for starting a pilot, but it does tell the story of a planned outreach. It provides a starting place to begin filling in the details about an outreach plan. Storyboards are also great for talking about a project with administrators or other stakeholders, providing a visual representation of what is going to happen at the outreach and what impact the outreach will have on a community. Such visualizations connect people to a solution in a more visceral way than do verbal explanations.

FIGURE 7.9 Storyboard

Storyboarding can sometimes make staff anxious if they feel their drawing skills do not pass muster. A rapid prototype allows you and your team to build out the solution and tell the outreach story without reliving any childhood traumas around artistic skills.

Rapid Prototyping

Rapid prototyping delivers similar results as storyboarding, providing a visual aid to tell a solution's story. We chose to prototype two different solutions for this exercise: at-home technology kits (see figure 7.10) and laptops at laundromats. Small teams were put together to work on each of the different solutions.

This was our second time prototyping the laundromat laptop outreach. The first prototype had focused more on the process and implementation rather than program specifics. For this prototype, the team looked at the

FIGURE 7.10 **Rapid Prototype: Tech Kits @ Home**

actual physical space, building the activity zones and explaining what would occur during the outreach. They expanded upon the earlier model, adding a small book collection in addition to the laptop lending station. Consideration was also given to the furniture choices and layout in the laundromat. At the end of the design time, team members told the story of their outreach, using the prototype as a visual aid. During the storytelling, they brought up influences from previous exercises. For example, they drew ideas from a potential thorn and discussed options for preventing theft of and damage to the laptops.

The second solution we prototyped was technology kits for the home. Staff members on this team built a sample kit using the supplies in their design thinking toolbox. The prototype included several different pieces of technology, such as an iPad and e-reader, that had been listed as part of the earlier mind map exercise; a Makey Makey (an electronic invention kit) and materials to build paper circuits; as well as project guides and activities for each of the different devices. Taking into consideration the importance of evaluation, the team also included a sample survey in the kit.

During the storytelling of this prototype, team members explained that the kit could come with lots of different types of technology or be broken into smaller kits that focused on just one element. They talked about how our teacher persona from the empathy map saw students and parents struggling to learn new technology, and about how the teachers also expressed a desire to integrate new technology into their curricula but rarely had enough time to do so. In developing the kit, the team would partner with teachers to create project guides that built off of classroom learning. The guides would be simple to follow, easing the frustration and struggles faced by families.

Cover Story Mockup

The Cover Story Mockup is another one of my favorite exercises as it looks at a solution from an entirely new perspective. Instead of showing the process or implementation of the solution, staff are driven to think about the outcomes of the outreach. In this exercise, we approached our solution as if we were journalists writing a cover story article about our library's outreach. If the outreach was successful enough that someone wanted to write a story about it, what would that journalist say? I like to use this as the final prototype exercise leading into the development of the pilot program. When building the plan for the pilot, we will focus on evaluation metrics, so the cover story mockup puts us into that outcomes mind-set, assisting us in projecting our goals for the outreach's success.

For this exercise, we chose two projects from our decision matrix board: laptops at the laundromat and technology kits for teachers. Each team brainstormed a real magazine that might write an article about the outreach program and then drew the magazine mastheads on the front of their article prototypes. They also added to the front of each magazine a cover image and title about the story featured inside (see figure 7.11). Opening up the magazine, each team then wrote the first paragraph of the featured story and highlighted outcomes.

This prototyping exercise further expanded our laptops at the laundromat outreach solution. We had learned some specifics about how we might build and run the outreach from our previous two prototyping exercises. Through the cover story mockup, we investigated which outcomes we wanted to see from this outreach. We identified a goal of fifteen patrons securing jobs within three months of participating in career classes at the laundromat. Also, our library wanted to see at least 75 percent of patrons feeling more confident about using laptops and navigating online.

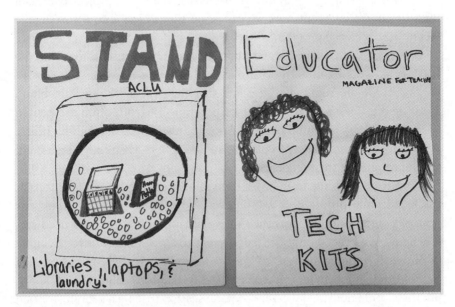

FIGURE 7.11 **Cover Story Mockups**

HOW DO WE TURN OUR PROTOTYPES INTO REAL-WORLD OUTREACH PROGRAMS?

Taking the time to discuss and draw out our goals in the cover story mockup was a quick way to set ourselves up for the pilot and evaluation stages of the design process. All of the prototyping exercises gave our team space to try out our outreach ideas without spending very much time or money. We were able to see what might or might not work before expending valuable staff time. We will often do multiple rounds of prototyping, sometimes using the same exercise repeatedly. An iterative cycle brings to the surface new ideas, challenges us to think outside the box, and lays the groundwork for us to beginning planning the pilot outreach program.

Piloting an Outreach Program

Pilots are often smaller-scale versions of the final program or focus on just one piece of a larger project, so we can quickly get them up and running. These trial runs give us permission to fail, iterate, adjust, and try again. Everything we learn from a pilot is discussed within our project team and used to inform us about how we can scale the project into a sustainable technology outreach program.

Pilots give us the opportunity to bring our prototype solutions into the real world, working directly with our patrons. We sometimes tell participants that we are running a pilot and that their feedback is invaluable in assisting our library in creating future programs. Patrons often are excited to be part of the planning process, knowing their opinions will be heard. People are also more likely to participate in surveys when they understand the importance of their feedback.

Our team built the framework for a pilot program using the laptops at the laundromat prototypes. Wanting to get up and running as quickly as possible, we aimed to connect with several laundromats in high-need service areas. We needed only one laundromat to agree to host us for a couple of outreach sessions in order to operate this pilot. At these pilot outreach events, our team members would bring out five laptops and Wi-Fi hot spots, but they would not run the career training session that we had brainstormed earlier in the prototype. Putting together that level of class would require a great deal of planning, so we chose not to include the lofty extras and instead focus on the core aspects of the outreach.

We use a pilot to gather information about the overall framework of a program. We think about the questions we need to have answered by the pilot, keeping in mind that each stage of the design process influences and builds on the previous one. Learning from the prototyping exercises informs the pilot, with the pilot becoming more detailed, adding extra layers, and answering new questions about what works or doesn't work. Lessons learned in the pilot stage assist us in creating a robust final program.

Some of the questions to answer in the pilot stage include these:

> How will we transport the laptops?
> Do we need power for the laptops at the laundromat?
> Where will people use the laptops?
> How will we handle laptop checkout? Will we offer laptop checkout?
> How much, if any, training will be given to participants?
> How long will people be allowed to use the laptops?
> What ages must people be to use the laptops?
> What do people want to learn?

Although piloting a program may seem more troublesome than simply jumping straight into planning the final outreach, it is actually a cost-effective process for ensuring that a program gets up and running smoothly. When we go right into planning a program without first prototyping and piloting it, we run the risk of getting stuck in an endless planning cycle. Staff can be hesitant to try their outreach program until everything is perfect. The traditional model of program creation creates an intense amount of pressure to get things right the first time. When staff invest so much time (and money) on a project, it can be very challenging to embrace failures and stay nimble enough to change things on the fly.

Technology-based programming of any kind is especially susceptible to failure on the first try. Buy-in can be expensive, with the high price of the technology adding to the costs for staff training and program planning. Design thinking gives us space to fail and try again. By working through this process, we identify potential barriers before they present themselves and create programming that is ready to handle any challenges as they come up. We become ready to respond rather than just react. The design process also sets us up to think about our outcomes from the very beginning, from understanding the problem we are trying to solve to determining how we will know that we are on the right track to solve it.

HOW DO WE KNOW IF OUR OUTREACH IS WORKING?

Evaluating the success of an outreach program is one of the most critical parts of the design process. How will we know if we are meeting our goals without assessing the program? Evaluation gives us the data needed to tell the story of our outreach, explaining to stakeholders the value of our work, showing us the impact our outreach has on participants, and ensuring we are on the right path to solving our problem.

Continuing with the laptops at the laundromat outreach program, our team had to ask, "How will we know if our program is working?" First, we had to go back to our "How might we . . . ?" problem statement. Our goal was to create more technology-curious communities. In our assessment, we made sure to ask the right questions and make observations that would tell us if our solution was actually solving our problem.

Looking back at our prototype exercises, we saw that we wanted participants to feel increased confidence using computers, for people to gain career skills, and to increase access to technology in high-needs neighborhoods. If we saw participants meeting these goals, then we would be successfully answering our "How might we . . . ?" question. Using the Outcomes Tracking Worksheet (see chapter 6), we brainstormed our target outputs and outcomes. Once we had targets outlined, we needed to choose the measurement tools we would use to see if we were meeting our goals. Our team decided to measure for these outputs and outcomes through surveys, speaking with participants, observation, and gathering basic program statistics. Here are our targets:

Outputs after six months:
> One hundred participants
> Twelve job training classes
> One thousand hours of laptop usage

> > Partnership with three laundromats
> > Sixty laptops in the field

Outcomes after six months:
> > Seventy-five percent of participants have an increase in confidence online.
> > Eighty percent of participants explored technology on their own after the outreach.
> > Five participants secured a new job.
> > Fifty percent of participants brought a new person with them to a second outreach.

Get out of the habit of measuring only how many people attend your outreach program. An outreach event where 1,000 people participated may not be as impactful as one with ten people in attendance. Through evaluation of your outcomes, you can tell the story of how your library transforms lives. Your outreach may not always be as successful as you originally thought it would be, but don't give up! Keep on iterating and you too can develop a technology-based outreach that makes a big impact in your community.

TECHNOLOGY OUTREACH IN PRACTICE

Real-World Case Studies

I t is one thing to dream and design outreach programming within the comfort of the library walls; it is quite another to actually implement a technology-based outreach program in the field. It is easy to feel alone and overwhelmed by potential challenges. This fear leads many people to never move forward with their outreach ideas. The design thinking process will give you a road map to successfully conquer that fear and take an outreach idea from prototype to real-world program.

The case studies in this chapter are all examples of technology-based outreach programs we implemented at the San José Public Library. You will find details on how we designed the outreach, specifics about what happened during the program, challenges we faced, and the lessons we learned. Learn from our mistakes, incorporate our work into your designs, and forge forward into your own technology-based outreach!

→ VIDEO MAKING AT THE SKATE PARK

Teenagers have famously been known as a challenging group to reach through library programming. Within groups of teens, some are regulars at the library and others will never step foot inside the library's doors. How do we reach those teens who never come to the library with programming that is of interest and value to them? Getting ourselves outside the library and going to the teens, instead of them coming to us, is a natural first step.

Using the stakeholder mapping exercise as part of our design thinking process, we identified a group of teens to target. The teens we planned to connect with spent the majority of their time at a local skate park. This skate park is located in a low-income area that has a high crime rate. In particular, the skate park was having problems with gang violence. To combat the problems, the local community center that ran the facility brought in a former gang member turned pastor to run regular operations. He was looking for any opportunity to partner with other organizations that could assist him in turning the skate park into a safe place for youth to hang out.

This partnership had a great deal of potential, but what were we going to do once we arrived? Our library wanted to connect these teens with technology of some kind. That is about all we knew getting started. As we began working through the design thinking process, we thought about what activities happen at a skate park. Videotaping tricks to share with friends and family online quickly came to the top of the list.

Our prototyped solution led us to believe we could empower the teens at the skate park through technology. We knew they often watched their favorite skaters online but did not have opportunities to make their own videos. Going out to the park with GoPro cameras, the technology used by experts in the field, would enable teens to learn new skills and expand their access to new technology.

Getting Started

After selecting our location, we identified the stakeholders we needed to work with in order to host our outreach. We connected with the pastor who ran the facility, meeting him on-site to learn the history of the skate park and to talk with several regular teen skaters.

When discussing the site's background, the manager explained that they had been having a lot of trouble with drug and alcohol use when he came on board. The park was constantly being spray-painted with gang signs. The manager began working directly with the teens to improve the site. He had local artists come in to create spray-painted artwork, and the gang tagging ended. Park staff began hosting competitions and getting to know the teens who skated there regularly. With these efforts, drug use and violence began decreasing. The teens became invested in the park and worked toward any effort that kept it open.

We also spoke to several teens during our initial visit. We explained what we were thinking of doing for the outreach, and they all seemed very interested in using the GoPros. They often used their phones to film themselves and friends skating, but that technology was limited in terms of creating high-quality, professional videos.

Building the Program

The park manager informed us that attendance varied highly from day to day. We agreed to come during a large skating competition, which would ensure us an audience. The park expected to host fifty to one hundred teens at the event. Music blasting and many boxes of pizza were sure ways to draw in a crowd of teenagers! During the event, the announcer would alert teens to our presence, inviting them to check out a camera.

With the basic details of the outreach sketched out, we began planning the specifics. First, we purchased ten GoPro cameras and harnesses in various sizes that could be worn on the chest or head. All these items were tagged with numbers so they could be easily identified and cataloged.

At this point, the cameras did not seem like a big enough learning opportunity. The teens had already been filming on their phones. We wanted them to walk away with new skills, not just new technology experiences. It is one thing to film, but the bigger lesson comes from editing a video and uploading it to the Internet to share. As such, we prepared four Toshiba Toughbooks. Each of the laptops was loaded with video-editing software and links to copyright-free music. We also connected Wi-Fi hot spots for Internet access.

During the gaining insights exercises that we did in preparation for the outreach, our team spoke to many teens about how they like to learn. One thing we discovered was that teens prefer to have light guidance instead of highly structured classes. To facilitate this learning style, we printed instructions on how to upload and edit videos to leave with each laptop.

Three librarians who were experienced with working with teens attended the outreach. They planned on bringing a large table to set up the laptops and to create a camera checkout station. In order to prevent theft, we decided to check out cameras to only those teens who had some kind of identification. We created a sign-up sheet that listed the equipment checked out and the teens' first and last names.

Outreach Specifics

Upon arrival at the skate park, our staff set up a table with laptops and cameras. To gain the teens' trust, one of our division managers grabbed his skateboard, strapped on a camera, and hit the ramps. He was able to skate around telling teens that they too could use the cameras.

In our Rose, Thorn, Bud exercise, we had identified theft as a potential risk. Our initial idea to prevent theft had been to check ID cards. Teens would give us their IDs to hold onto while they were out skating with the cameras. This proved very quickly not to work at all. None of the teens were carrying any identification. There were a few minutes of panic, but our team brainstormed quickly, deciding just to let them write down their names; and then we took photos of them using our cellphones—an idea that turned out to be awful as the photos were low quality. In retrospect, it would have been fine just to have them give us their names. We did not have any problems with theft. All the teens were excited about the opportunity to use the new technology, and everything was brought back to us promptly with no issues.

The good news was that teens were checking out the equipment to use during their skate time. We did run into complications because they weren't just free skating. Instead, there was a competition taking place, so most of their attention was focused on that instead of on using the cameras. They checked out the cameras thinking that they would have time to use them and then came back shortly after to tell us they were next in the competition so could not participate in the full outreach program. Because there was such a rush, we did not have a lot of time to do any kind of instruction. However,

Concerns about theft may be a major hurdle for your library. If possible, build a loss rate into your budget. Pilot your program with a smaller number of devices or equipment before investing heavily in something that might get stolen. In some cases, it may be possible to secure devices to a table. Alternatively, you can plan the outreach so that staff are constantly monitoring the technology.

the teens who did borrow cameras for the full twenty-minute time slot consistently came back to tell us about all the cool tricks they had filmed.

Although the cameras were used a lot, the editing portion of the outreach was not very successful. Rendering and editing video take a long time. Teens sat down to edit, but when it was not happening fast enough, they left to go skate, which is why they were there. Our Wi-Fi hot spots did not provide speeds fast enough to upload to YouTube either. So, we told teens to leave their videos on the computer and we would upload them later. However, we did not realize the computers had Deep Freeze installed on them. This meant that when they were shut down, everything that had been uploaded was deleted.

Challenges

It was difficult to decide when we should go to the park to run our pilot program. Attendance ebbed and flowed throughout the day and week. There was not a set schedule when we could rely on teens being there.

We also knew that we had to gain the trust of the users. How were we going to relate to this user group and show them that we have something of value to offer them? Trust is earned. We were going to have to present ourselves in a way that demonstrated to the teens that we could be trusted.

"Won't everything just get stolen?" was a common question posed to us, especially at the administrative level. Bringing expensive technology into a low-income area and then letting it get strapped to the helmet of a teen who is skating around can be nerve-racking for some. We had to think about what measures to put in place to ensure equipment did not get stolen and what to do if it did walk away.

Lessons Learned

Test the Technology

Understanding the limitations of the technology you plan to use for an outreach is important. We did not try out the Wi-Fi hot spots on-site before the event. That meant we did not know the speed of the Internet connection. There was also no trial run for the editing process. No one was aware that it takes thirty minutes for a video to render or that the whole editing process could be a program in and of itself. Spending time testing out the technology before the outreach would have enabled our staff to adjust the program accordingly.

Know the Audience

The teens we interacted with had a blast using the GoPro cameras. However, they did not get the full value we had anticipated due to the large event happening at the same time. We focused on quantity over quality, getting excited about the possibility of a large audience at a skate competition. Our time would have been better spent visiting the skate park several times, talking with teens to figure out when they go there and how they spend their time. This also could help to build trust with our target audience.

Visit the Same Location Multiple Times

Making this location the site of regular outreach efforts would provide staff with the opportunity to expand into a substantive learning opportunity rather than a technology excitement program. A storyboarding component had been brainstormed in the prototype stage but not implemented during the pilot.

Storyboarding teaches about how films are made and the nature of telling a story with a beginning, middle, and end. Having big boards available for storyboarding at the skate park would give teens an opportunity to learn from their peers and build up excitement for our next visit. While building their film's story, teens would be able to visit a computer to watch inspirational skate videos from professionals.

Other outreach days would be earmarked for filming. We would label the equipment and have big boards available to show stills and give hints about how to experiment with the video equipment. During these skating days, staff would inform teens about the upcoming editing days.

During editing sessions, computers would be available with easy-to-use editing software and a set of predownloaded songs. The editing process should not take more than an hour to complete. Although it is great to have fast Wi-Fi, this might not always be possible at an outreach location. To prepare for that possibility, completed videos would be saved on external drives and uploaded back at the library. A library hashtag could be used to easily find and share the teens' videos later.

→ POP-UP MOBILE MAKERSPACES

The cities we live in are mostly designed without our input. The majority of citizens are unable to have a say in urban planning. City council meetings are held during the workweek, generally at inconvenient times for other working adults. How can we expect to have engaged citizens, active and interested in the place they live, when they have no ability to shape what happens there?

In recent years, stakeholders in San José have been deeply involved in trying to solve the quandary of how to create an engaged citizenry. Specifically, our city has been looking into how to make downtown more livable and playable. We have been asking ourselves, "How can we transform downtown into a place where people want to hang out?"

The San José Public Library was approached by a local artist, Corinne Okada Takara, who was active in trying to answer this question. She wanted to develop a project that gave members of the public an opportunity to share their visions about underutilized downtown spaces. Corinne had the idea to go directly into these underutilized spaces, setting up pop-up makerspaces where we could connect directly with the public, sourcing their ideas on how to improve downtown. All the ideas gathered at these pop-up events would then be shared with downtown stakeholders.

To elicit ideas from the public, Corinne envisioned using mobile makerspaces with technology that allowed people to prototype their ideas in a physical format. The setup would teach design thinking skills and help people to think creatively. The pop-ups would also engage local youths by offering them paid positions through which they could become ambassadors of civic engagement for their generation.

We moved forward with the project, first, by soliciting grant funding from the Knight Foundation. Then, following the design thinking process, we developed our "How might we . . . ?" problem statement to inform our program planning. Our team asked, "How might we engage a wide range of San José citizens in new ways of discussing urban public space design while creating a platform that enlivens underutilized public spaces?"

Getting Started

Sometimes library staff are the geniuses behind a new program, and sometimes an engaged member of the community comes up with an idea. For this particular project, we were fortunate enough for it to be the latter. We love opportunities to engage with our patrons beyond just finding their favorite books for them! Corinne, a successful artist in the Bay Area working with the community through art and technology, had spent a great deal of time teaching 3-D printing, urban space design, and place making. Through her work, she identified a need for members of the general public to have a voice in their city and dreamt up an innovative way to capture that voice.

Corinne had previously held some mini pop-up events, and upon seeing how engaged people were at these events, she began to seek avenues for expansion. She connected with the Knight Foundation, who suggested the library as a potential partner for her project. When Corinne approached us with the idea, we were excited for the opportunity to move out into the community with technology.

With the grant funding in place, we set out to begin figuring out how to solve our problem statement, separating it into two tasks: "How are we going to engage a wide range of citizens?" and "How are we going to enliven the underutilized spaces we choose for pop-ups in the downtown area?"

Building the Program

This outreach program had many moving parts that had to come together in order to be successful. This was not a small, one-time event but, rather, a set of outreaches that would span several months. We first had to identify where the outreaches would take place, securing the appropriate permissions to set up each time. Then, we had to plan the activities that would take place.

> **Deciding where you will have your outreach is one of the most important parts of determining its success.** Visit the space during the time you plan on hosting the event to see if it has the right vibe. Find out if any permits are required. Talk to local business owners. Scope it out to the best of your ability before showing up for your outreach event.

Once we knew what would happen at the outreach, we had to have furniture designed and built. This was the first time our staff would be using technology such as 3-D printers, which meant a lot of training had to take place. Our library had never done an outreach series like this before, so we also had to enlist the help of our marketing department to get the word out.

Choosing the Sites

Our first step was deciding where we should have the pop-ups. The project aimed not only to gather public opinions about enlivening downtown but also to generate activity in those spaces. The pop-ups would act as events to engage people in downtown activities, something sorely lacking in San José. We sought out areas that were not being used to their full potential but where there was still some foot traffic.

We initially chose three sites to host the pop-ups, with each hosting an event on at least three separate occasions. We chose the San Pedro Square Farmers Market as our starting location. The space where the market is held is underutilized at all times other than when the market is operating. We decided to host our pop-up during the market's open hours to ensure foot traffic and make for an easy entry point for staff to become comfortable with the setup.

The next site chosen was Parque de los Pobladores. However, when we checked in with the Office of Cultural Affairs, we were told that it was unavailable for our use due to an activation event planned with architect Teddy Cruz. We had to find an alternative site quickly since the dates for our event had already been selected. Corinne suggested using the large plaza in front of the Dr. Martin Luther King Jr. Library as the space is rarely used for anything except walking into the building. In addition, the library is shared with San José State University, giving us an opportunity to expand our audience reach and engage with students.

The last selected site was the San José Repertory Plaza. This spot had the least amount of regular foot traffic, especially during the weekends (when we planned to operate the pop-ups). The plaza is located near a light rail stop and acts as a thoroughfare for people moving to their final destinations. As we investigated setting up in the space, we found that permitting was required. We worked with the city to have inspections done and paid a permitting fee to set up for the pop-up events.

Outreach Activities

Next, we developed questions to ask participants to solve through their prototype designs:

1. What do we need more of downtown?
2. What do we need less of downtown?
3. What are ways we can create opportunities for play, rest, recreation, privacy, or connection?
4. How might we invite people to linger in this space?

Our team then planned the activities for the pop-up events. We offered several different levels of participation at these events. People could choose to create cardboard prototypes and photograph them on small stages with a photograph of the actual program space as a backdrop. Participants could also use Tinkercad to do a CAD (computer-aided design) rendering of their ideas for structures that enhanced the public space; models were 3-D printed on-site and kept at the library for display at future pop-ups. We also supplied everyone's favorite design thinking tools: a ton of sticky notes and markers for people to brainstorm ideas; the ideas generated were posted for others participants to see and build upon. Last, we made available an online survey to gather data about people's wants and needs for downtown spaces.

Furniture

All these activities required the use of furniture. Corinne had previously seen an image of a rolling bench and began imagining furniture with large wheelbarrow wheels that could be used to engage the public at pop-up outreach events. She then created her own 3-D printer pop-up cart, taking it to community events to teach about the power of 3-D printers. The success of the cart led her to begin sketching plans for a set of mobile furniture that could be wheeled out to events to be set up in a variety of layouts.

Our pop-up furniture set consisted of a 3-D printer cart (for an example, see figure 8.1 in the Marketing section), prototyping tables, display cases, benches for people to sit on, and double-facing

> **If you want to engage lots of people at your outreach, offer various levels of activities.** Plan one thing for the casual passerby and another for the highly engaged.

The space you choose for outreach is important. People are influenced by their surroundings. Use that fact to your advantage! Brainstorm ways to blend your technology with projects that reflect the space you plan to set up in.

chalkboards/corkboards. All the furniture included space to place large colorful umbrellas that invited people to sit in the shade while participating. We found a local fabricator, one who could work on a tight schedule, to construct all the furniture quickly.

Staffing

This project presented an exciting opportunity for staff to get out of their branches or departments and experiment with a new service model. We put out a call to all our staff asking for any interested librarians and clerks. Those who expressed interest answered a few questions about their qualifications and why they were interested. Those who submitted applications were interviewed to see who would make the best fit for the outreach. During interviews, I looked for flexibility, critical-thinking skills, and a passion for technology.

> **Every library is different, and sometimes paying teens can be tricky!** Make sure to connect with your finance department to determine the best methods for making this happen.

Part of the project plan included bringing on board teen interns to work each of the outreach events. Money was set aside in the grant to pay a small stipend to all teens for their participation. Paying the teens was important to us. Unpaid internships or volunteer opportunities present barriers to low-income youth who are required to work over the summer to help support their families. Providing a small stipend helped us to bring on board a diverse group of teens and was a source of empowerment for the participating youths.

To recruit volunteers, we asked teens to submit online applications and then conducted interviews with all interested teens. Inviting all the teens for interviews gave them an opportunity to practice that skill set, even if they were not selected for the final project. Corinne explained at the beginning of the project how important it was not just to engage the people who came to the pop-ups but also to teach new skills to a set of young people. The teens were a critical part of the outreach's success.

Six teens were chosen from the pool of applicants. We looked for a variety of different qualities when selecting the final group. The final volunteers demonstrated interest in technology and civic engagement, they were available to attend all trainings and outreach events, and they came from neighborhoods throughout the city. Most important, we sought out teens who were excited about participating!

Training

Prior to the event, our staff and teens attended several trainings. The first training session was a design thinking workshop led by Corinne and hosted at The Tech Museum of Innovation (aka The Tech) in San José. Everyone also went to a maker workshop that focused on urban design reflections through prototyping as well as workshops for learning the CAD tool Tinkercad, how to operate the 3-D printers, and how to solder.

Marketing

At San José Public Library, we are extremely fortunate to have an amazing in-house marketing team. Our graphic designer created a logo and brand style for the outreach events that we used in developing handouts for the events, promotional fliers (see figure 8.1), instructional fliers, and shirts. Everything was bright pink, drawing the attention of even the far-away passerby. Pink umbrellas and matching staff shirts made the pop-ups hard to miss. The engaging marketing materials also served as a tool to draw people into underutilized spaces where they did not normally linger. The marketing team also promoted the events through various social media accounts. Fliers were distributed in libraries and at various businesses throughout the downtown area.

> **Ensure that all staff are trained and comfortable with the technology well in advance of the outreach.** Having at least one person who can troubleshoot will help to ensure a successful event.

FIGURE 8.1 **Pop-Up Makerspace Outreach Flier**

Supplies

I worked with Corinne to drill down into the nitty-gritty details of what supplies were required for the outreach. The first item on our list was two 3-D

Don't have your own design team? Don't stress! Flex your creative muscles and make your own fliers. They do not need to be fancy to catch the eye of a passerby. Think of the audience that gathers at your outreach. Where else do these people go in your town? Visit these locations to drop off fliers and talk to potential participants.

printers. One of these always went out as part of the pop-ups, and the other lived at the library for use in making prints of objects participants designed during the outreach.

Then, we brainstormed the best way to get power to the mobile 3-D printer. Regular gasoline generators are loud and smelly, so we decided instead on a solar generator that could be charged at the library before an event.

In addition to the 3-D printers and solar generator, we needed design thinking prototyping kits. We purchased and/or found an assortment of items: bottle caps, straws, rubber mats, plastic cups, fabric, and so forth. We also included modeling clay, scissors, tape, LEDs, batteries, motors, and anything else we could get our hands on that could be used to build prototypes. Other necessary supplies included laptops and Wi-Fi hot spots.

We had multiple pairs of eyes look over our lists before the outreach events to see if we had missed anything. As the pop-ups began to run, staff discovered new additions that we purchased on the fly to continue improving subsequent outreach events.

Outreach Specifics

The pop-ups were scheduled to take place at various downtown locations from July to September. We planned to visit each location at least three times. Scheduling multiple visits in the same location invited people to return to the site the following week to continue building upon their ideas or to see the prototypes other people had developed. Because most of the 3-D printing was done at the library, not at the outreach, participants could come back again the next week to see the physical manifestations of their CAD designs.

The San Pedro Square Farmers Market and the Repertory Plaza hosted the pop-ups three times each. The Dr. Martin Luther King Jr. Library hosted the outreach six times. During the summer months, two other events also occurred that were outside of our initial scope: a Parking Day event (during which parking meter spaces were turned into mini parks) and a Mini Maker Faire. Each of the events was three hours long.

Teen volunteers signed up for shifts at the beginning of the summer. They met the librarian and clerk at the library an hour before each event to help load the furniture onto an interlibrary delivery truck. Everyone walked over to the outreach spot together to wait for the truck to deliver the furniture.

The furniture was set up in the spot, supplies were unpacked, and the 3-D printer and laptops were turned on. The display cases were loaded up with all the 3-D prints that had been designed at previous outreach events. The sticky notes from previous pop-ups in that particular space were also kept on the display boards to serve as inspiration for those choosing to participate.

People stopping by the pop-up got an explanation of the project and an invitation to contribute their ideas about improving downtown. We designed instruction cards to help educate people about the urban design process. Staff and volunteers assisted participants with whichever activity they wanted to complete.

Throughout the events, staff and volunteers captured photos to post on social media. In an effort to share our findings with downtown stakeholders, we gathered the photos and the data from surveys and told our outreach story in a printed book. Books were cataloged in the library collection and distributed to stakeholders.

Challenges

Our pop-ups had a lot of pieces that needed to be put together for the events to be successful. One of the first things we had to figure out was what to

Use your brainstorming skills to dream up all the possible items you might need for the outreach. Do a trial run before you leave. Invite coworkers or patrons to try activities in the library. Discovering you are missing something *before* you arrive is always desirable. Be prepared to not get it all right the first time. Reflect on the experience when you return to the library and iterate.

> **The more moving** parts you have for an outreach, the more challenges you have to be prepared for. You can never anticipate all the challenges that might occur during an outreach, but you can prepare yourself by using exercises such as Rose, Thorn, Bud to lessen your chances of getting caught off guard. If you are doing multiple outreaches, be sure to take time after each one to evaluate and think about what challenges came up during the program. Use the exercises in chapter 6 of this book to iterate and improve your outreach as needed.

do with all the amazing furniture we had built for the pop-ups. It took up a personal office's worth of space. I negotiated for room near my office that we could dedicate to the storage of the furniture. It actually took up so much space that the library donated it to Corinne after the project so she could continue using it for outreach events.

Once the furniture arrived, we discovered that it was not quite as mobile as we originally had envisioned. The wheels were small and the handles too short. Without having time to rebuild, we made what modifications we could and tried rolling it out to the first event. That proved to be a fruitless effort. With all the bumps in the road, and huge furniture pieces, we quickly discovered that we needed another option for transportation. We worked with our interbranch delivery drivers to arrange times for them to drop off and pick up the furniture for each of the outreach events. Our mobile pop-up was not exactly as mobile as we had hoped!

The biggest challenge our staff faced was getting people involved. How do you get people who are walking by to stop to have a meaningful interaction with you? Our bright pink umbrellas and shirts caused lots of people to stop, but they often thought we were advertising something related to breast cancer awareness. (Next time we might want to go with a different bright color!) Our on-site librarian made signs displaying our library's name for all the furniture to help combat this misunderstanding.

There was a lot going on at each of the pop-ups. People who dropped by were presented with a plethora of options for participating. Did they want to leave a quick sticky note? Fill out a survey? Learn how to use Tinkercad and design a 3-D model? Build their own prototype model? Learn how a 3-D printer works? Some of these options require a lot of time and people passing by were usually on their way to do something else. The nature of the pop-up was to invite those walking by to share their visions, not necessarily to draw in the public just for that one outreach event. Scaling down to just one or two activities per event may have prevented this choice overload.

Our on-site librarian also quickly discovered that people making CAD designs were not very good at it after learning only the basics. She spent a great deal of time back at the library fixing their files to ensure they printed successfully.

Lessons Learned

Assess Project Mobility

For this project, we had specialized furniture that was supposed to allow us to cart our whole outreach kit around the downtown area on foot. Yet, it turns out that we did not have enough experience in designing furniture or time to iterate on the designs to make our furniture truly mobile.

> **All outreach requires you to be mobile.** When you are planning your outreach, think about your mobility needs. Will you be walking or driving to the outreach? If you are driving, what kind of vehicle are you taking? How big is that vehicle? What are the library's rules about transporting supplies in your personal vehicle?

Using technology added a whole other level of complexity. We knew that we would not have power in any of the locations. Regular generators are easy to transport, but they make a lot of noise and create pollution. Solar generators are fantastic but can weigh more than 100 pounds; they also have large panels that can be cumbersome to travel with. We decided to use a solar generator and found that with an overnight charge it would last through the whole outreach without needing to deploy the panels. It was still very difficult to move around. Since the furniture design did not allow us to move to the sites on the street, we utilized our branch delivery trucks. The drivers were able to lift the generator in and out of the trucks, relieving this burden on the outreach staff.

> **Consider the activity you will be doing.** If people need to use laptops, will they be sitting or standing? Any tables set up for participants to use will need to be the appropriate height to meet accessibility guidelines.

It can be tempting to want to do everything all at once. Perhaps your library just got a new grant or donation and you have outfitted yourself with all the latest and greatest technology tools. You now have a library filled to the brim with 3-D printers, VR glasses, Arduino kits, soldering irons, sewing machines, and more. You may be inclined to put it into one great touring roadshow, letting everyone choose whatever technology they want to play with that day. Although show-and-tell technology programs have their place, even they should be focused so that you can identify the learning outcomes.

For future outreaches, we would plan to do a dry run, moving all the furniture and equipment before the day of the outreach to help reduce stress on the day of the outreach. Instead of scrambling to fix the transportation problems after the outreach events had begun, we would have found a solution early on.

Be Focused

Our Pop-Up Mobile Makerspaces program taught us that offering a lot of activities is complicated and stressful for staff. Technology is not yet seamless and has many more opportunities for failure than a standard library arts and crafts program.

Many outreach programs take place at locations where people are going to be passing by. If there are a myriad of options, they will likely be overwhelmed by all the choices, choosing to do nothing at all instead. We had a lot of activities at each of our events, and even with a robust staff, it was challenging to guide someone through the entire process in a short amount of time.

Think about levels of complexity. Can you set up quick lessons for those who just want to experience the technology quickly without frustration? What programming will be available for those who want to explore in more depth? Hand-hold the beginners while giving others the freedom to play.

Stick with Simple Technology

Although our 3-D printer drew in crowds, it was slow and difficult to use. The simple technology we brought out with us was the most useful in engaging people. Initially, we planned to teach soldering but ran into some challenges in the implementation. Instead, we brought copper tape, LEDs, and pager motors. People combined these items with clay, cardboard, LEGOs, and a whole host of other simple prototyping tools. Our staff taught circuits and civic design all in one shot.

> **Sometimes the most simple of your technology can be used in creative ways that teach real skills but may not be flashy.** Libraries can spend minimal amounts of money on simple technologies, such as paper circuits, which have a huge range of options for exploration.

→ MAKER[SPACE]SHIP

We all know there are portions of our communities that never step foot inside our libraries. It is one of the key reasons we do outreach! Since the 1850s, librarians have been going out into their communities to provide direct service. As Mary Titcomb, the librarian who created the first bookmobile in the United States, has said, "The book goes to the man, not waiting for the man to come to the book."[1] In the twenty-first century, why limit ourselves to just books? Our library began thinking about a space that wasn't about book literacy but instead focused on helping our patrons learn how to solve problems using technology.

Positioned as it is in the heart of Silicon Valley, our city is home to many of the world's leaders in technology. Yet, many of our citizens live without access to the tools being created in their own backyard. Our library realized that we could play a key role in expanding access to these tools and to STEAM (science, technology, engineering, arts, mathematics) skills. We began to ask ourselves, "How are we going to bring STEAM and maker education to the community?"

Our first idea to increase STEAM skills and access to technology was one that many libraries have adopted in recent years: putting makerspaces in our buildings. Libraries around the world are offering an incredible amount of programming, teaching everything from 3-D modeling to costume design. However, we were not able to outfit all of our branches with a full makerspace. We also recognized that we have a large population that does not visit the library. Meeting people where they are, in a space where they feel safe, could help us connect people with technology and bridge the digital divide.

We saw an opportunity to take the traditional bookmobile model that has worked for more than 100 years and flip it upside down. We would engage with our community in spaces where we hadn't ventured to do technology-based programming. We began dreaming up a mobile makerspace and asked ourselves, "How might we inspire people to solve problems creatively?"

Getting Started

We began our design process in the typical way, with only a big concept. We knew that we wanted to build a mobile makerspace but were unsure of the design or programming. We didn't know any specifics at the beginning of the design process or even what problem we were trying to solve. Among our library staff were only design thinking novices so we chose to bring in an expert.

We applied for and received a grant from the Pacific Library Partnership, allocating the grant funds toward hiring a design consultant. Parker Thomas, then Managing Partner at Mirus Labs, now Executive Fellow at FUSE Corps, and design thinking consultant extraordinaire, was a natural fit for our team. Parker came to us with years of experience working with educational institutions to set up their makerspaces. He assisted us in using many of the same exercises outlined in this book to help us design our mobile makerspace.

Once Parker was on board we assembled our project team. The first group we brought together was nearly all management. This seemed like a

Don't be afraid to draw. Processing a big board dense with text is difficult. Your mind will be able to more easily differentiate between ideas when they are represented by pictures.

good fit at the beginning, though as we moved further along in the process, we realized a need for staff who interacted with our patrons more directly. Since design thinking is a flexible practice, we shifted the team to one with frontline staff instead of just administration.

In addition to the staff team, we created a teen project team. Similar to the Pop-Up Mobile Makerspaces project, we created an application and recruited a group of teens to work on the project in parallel with the staff team. One of our teen librarians led this effort. The teens performed exercises similar to those undertaken by the staff team, and the librarian reported on their progress at our staff meetings. Because the teen meetings were held on the weekends, it was difficult to have the group work together throughout the entire process. Instead, the teens came in toward the end of the design phase to do a working group session with staff. At this meeting, the physical space was designed using the knowledge that had been gained in previous sessions by both groups.

Building the Program

Our first step in the design process was to gain insights from the community, to connect with them to build our empathy. We did the Stakeholder Mapping exercise to figure out with whom we were going to talk. Then, we brainstormed what questions to ask them. Our staff decided to connect with several different user groups:

> › Youths (teens and tweens)
> › Teachers
> › Parents
> › Library staff
> › Learners in our adult reading program

Team members chose different stakeholder groups to interview, with the teens interviewing their peers. Everyone was encouraged to record their interviews, which was a huge help later on, as I was able to listen to all the interviews and draw the themes I heard on sticky notes. By compiling all this data, our team was able to create a visual map of all the feedback we had received. Together we grouped similar items, identifying broad themes across user groups.

Now that we knew what people wanted, we could define our problem. Our plan had to be about more than just building a vehicle, just like any outreach is about more than just showing off a piece of technology. We asked ourselves what outcomes we were trying to achieve. Our team processed the learning from the gaining insights exercise, coupling it with our own aspirations and potential barriers. From there, we were able to develop our problem statement: "How might we inspire people to solve problems creatively?"

After developing our problem statement, we moved into brainstorming solutions. Rather than designing the physical space first, we thought about what was going to happen in the space. Our physical design would be based off of the programmatic requirements. The brainstorming sessions started with these programs. What was going to happen on the bus?

Using the design thinking prototyping exercises, we developed a set of potential programming options. We then had to pilot these in the community. As we piloted programs, we made notes about what worked and what did not. Right away we discussed the elements that would influence our physical design.

From the lessons learned during the prototyping and the interviews, we began brainstorming a list of vehicle requirements. Using this list, we broke into small groups to do prototypes of the vehicle's final design. As the project manager, I then took these sketches and met with the city's fleet department staff to turn the prototypes into real-world vehicles. They assisted us in creating a request for proposal (RFP) and handled the bid process. (For more details about the Maker[Space]Ship design process, see the guidebook at sjpl.org/mobileguide.)

Once the bidding process was over and a vendor was selected, construction could begin! As the vehicle was being constructed, we began work on the other elements of the project, focusing in on the programming. Anyone can build something shiny and stock it full of technology. True learning will happen only if there is thoughtful and engaging programming.

Building your own mobile technology vehicle? Check out *On the Road with Outreach,* edited by Jeannie Dilger-Hill and Erica MacCreaigh, for a detailed request for purchase example and lots of specifics on how to build your technology-mobile.

Programming

A call went out asking any interested librarians to join a STEAM programming design team. A small group of five librarians, including myself, began working to design a set of programs that could be used on the vehicle. First, we created a program template (see figure 8.2). The template ensured that every program was easy to replicate and met a set of preidentified standards.

Title:

Description:

Marketing Blurb:

Estimated Length (indicate if multiple sessions):

Target Age:

Max Group Size:

Suggested Staff:

Materials:

Measurable Outcomes/Method for Evaluation:

Learning Objectives (Common Core and
Next Generation Science Standards):

Instructions:

Adaptation Needs for Branch:

External Resources (books or websites):

Presentation Materials:

Takeaways/Handouts:

FIGURE 8.2 **Outreach Program Template**

> **Search for places where people already gather.** Trying to get people to come out to a place just for your outreach can be challenging. Build off audiences and relationships that already exist.

The standards we put in place for ourselves included learning objectives and measurable outcomes. The bus itself is a confined space holding up to twenty people at one time. If the only metric for determining success was how many people attended, we would be left in quite the bind.

Because we knew the bus would be serving K–12 students, we also made sure that every program aligned with state and/or national educational standards. When approaching schools we could explain to teachers how the learning that took place on the bus enhanced what was happening in their classrooms.

Programming was created for all ages. Each month, the team met and decided on a different theme around which to build programming. One month it might be a particular piece of technology, such as a vinyl cutter; another month it might be a topic, such as engineering. Everyone worked around the same theme, with each person taking on a different age group (from preschool to seniors).

Bus Stops

As with any outreach, we first had to determine where we were going to go. With whom would we partner? What places would best serve the audience we were attempting to reach? At the start of the Maker[Space]Ship project, we wanted to find a variety of different places that included partners who were easy to work with. Because the staff needed to get familiar with the regular operations during these initial visits, we wanted places that would give us quick wins.

We created a list of all the potential partners and sites we might want to visit by reflecting back on our "How might we . . . ?" question and the information gained from connecting with our stakeholders. Sites included low-income housing facilities, senior centers, after-school programs, parks, community centers, urban farms, and churches. Armed with a measuring tape and camera, we drove around to potential sites to see if the bus could park safely at those locations. Some spots were crossed off the list before we ever reached out to the partner organization—no need to get someone excited about a visit from the Maker[Space]Ship only to find out that there is no way to park the bus on-site.

Strong partnerships are vital to the health of any outreach. We wanted to be able to talk to our partners about what we would be able to offer them and what they would be able to offer us. We created a template (see chapter 2, figure 2.2) to use during conversations with partners. After a meeting, we can evaluate the information gathered to determine if the partnership is a good fit for both organizations.

With partnerships solidified, a schedule began to take shape (see figure 8.3). We created letters to deliver to partners in advance of the visits that outlined their responsibilities, such as reserving a parking space. Partnerships are two-way streets. To be effective, each party has to deliver on their promises. With a large outreach operation, like a mobile vehicle, this becomes even more important. Technology outreach of any kind usually has extra layers of complexity that need to come together for success.

Supplies

With a schedule built and programming designed, we had to start purchasing all the supplies. Our staff team spent many hours looking at the data gathered from our gaining insights exercise. What did people want to do on board? What kinds of technology were they interested in interacting with? What supplies would we need to run the programming we had already developed?

Our team used design thinking brainstorming exercises to come up with the list of supplies we needed. We gathered sticky notepads and markers, furiously writing down all the ideas we could and sticking them on the wall. Together we built upon one another's ideas, creating a fleshed-out

Consider how many people might attend your outreach event. How do you want them to interact with the technology? Having only one piece of technology may not be enough to serve the needs of your community.

list of possible items to put on the bus. Items ranged from regular office supplies to high-tech tools.

The service model for the bus, to break down access barriers and to serve our low-income communities, influenced how many of each item we

Date	Time	Program	Location	Attendance	Primacy Age
1/5/2017	10:30 am	From Cow to Toast: Butter Making	Southside Community Center	19	Preschool
1/5/2017	12:30 pm	Wearable Tech: LED Brooch	Southside Community Center	7	Adult
1/6/2017	10:00 am	Wearable Tech: LED Brooch	Midtown Senior Apartments	12	Adult
1/10/2017	2:00 pm	Sketch and Play: Make Music with Makey Makey	Don de Dios Apartments	19	School Age
1/11/2017	10:30 am	From Cow to Toast: Butter Making	Calabazas Preschool	13	Preschool
1/12/2017	4:00 pm	Makey Makey	Guadalupe Church	60	School Age
1/14/2017	10:00 am	3-D Print Pens	Lake Cunningham Park	35	School Age
1/18/2017	10:30 am	From Cow to Toast: Butter Making	Roosevelt Community Center	21	Preschool
1/18/2017	12:30 pm	Wearable Tech: LED Brooch	Roosevelt Community Center	19	Adult
1/19/2017	10:30 am	Healthy Eating (partner)	Southside Community Center	23	Preschool

FIGURE 8.3 Maker[Space]Ship Outreach Schedule

Being able to fit all your supplies into an outreach vehicle is not something to be taken lightly. Space is limited when you do not have your handy storage closet nearby. When you go mobile, consider how much space will be available, and then make the best use out of what you have.

purchased. We wanted every station in the bus to have its own technology. We did not want any of the participants to have to wait in line; everyone should be able to do the activities together.

Once we had our supply list, we began purchasing. It felt like Christmas every day in my office for a few months! We knew that not all the supplies would live on board the bus and found additional storage for the items. As items came in, we unboxed and inventoried everything for easy access later.

We measured every single nook and cranny on our bus. Then, we went on many runs to the hardware store to purchase a wide assortment of different plastic storage containers. We wanted to make sure we could load all the materials we might need onto the bus before leaving for our stop for the day. Organized storage also gave staff easy access to supplies when they were not on the bus.

Logistics

A mobile outreach vehicle is likely the most intensive of all the technology-based outreach initiatives we could have chosen to undertake. We had to determine a staffing model, build a web page, create a marketing package and social media accounts, and get our staff trained to drive the new thirty-nine-foot bus!

We decided to have the bus operate under our centralized programming department. The librarians and clerical staff established partnerships, created the vehicle's route, developed and implemented the programming, and

Being organized is a lifesaver! Label your supplies and keep a running inventory so you can order replacements as needed. Nothing is worse than arriving at your outreach only to find something is missing.

> **Outreach is exhausting!** Make sure to build in enough time for setup, breakdown, and staff breaks.

evaluated services. Our bus currently operates about fifteen program hours a week, Monday through Saturday.

Outreach Specifics

"The Maker[Space]Ship is an innovative mobile workshop that overcomes access barriers in San José to foster creative ideas, connect people with technology, and encourage problem solving, collaboration, and discovery." This mission statement was derived from the original problem statement ("How might we inspire people to solve problems creatively?") and the work we did when talking to our stakeholders and prototyping programs. The whole service model is built off this mission statement; it is what drives program creation and the site selection.

So, what needed to happen to get the Maker[Space]Ship on the road? For successful outreach to occur, a lot had to happen behind the scenes. A full-service programming vehicle like the Maker[Space]Ship was the type of outreach that seemed like a full-time job in and of itself. Our librarians had to design programs, build the schedule, and deliver the outreach.

When building the Maker[Space]Ship, we purchased a wide range of technology and supplies for flexibility in future programming. Librarians have a lot of choice in selecting what will happen on board. Staff can also bring on partners who are interested in delivering their own programming. The library can provide the space and materials while the partners lend their expertise. This partnership model has been used several times with great success.

Most outreach programs must function with limited staff, so we try to find people who can think on their feet! Most often we are able to accommodate only two staff on board. For bigger outreach events, we can expand the area of our bus to the outside as well, with an awning, monitor, and speaker system. Having this flexibility enables two unique types of outreach setups for the Maker[Space]Ship.

The first type of outreach is at venues where we will have a set audience (see figure 8.4). This could be a senior center or a school. It is a location

TITLE: SCRIBBLE BOT CHALLENGE

Description
Participants will design and test their own small devices made from recycled parts that will generate a unique drawing on paper. Scribbling machines are motorized contraptions that move in unusual ways and leave a mark to trace their paths. They are made of simple materials and set in motion by the vibrating hobby motor, causing them to bounce, spin, bump, and move in interesting ways.

Marketing Blurb
Have you ever wondered what makes some objects move? Bring your curiosity along to upcycle commonly found items and create your very own motorized drawing machine!

Estimated Length: 1 hour
Target Age: 6–12 years
Materials:

Max Group Size: 20
Suggested Staffing: 2

- Hobby motor (1.5–3 V in size)
- Alligator clip wires
- Weight (e.g., large binder clips, erasers, clay, hot-melt glue stick)
- Attachments (thick rubber bands, masking tape)
- Recyclable containers (yogurt cups, strawberry boxes, plastic cups, etc.)
- Washable markers
- Batteries (AA, AAA, lithium batteries)
- Decorative elements (googly eyes, pipe cleaners, LEDs with lithium batteries)
- Butcher paper or poster board

Measurable Outcomes
Participants will be able to identify the parts of a scribble bot and will have created a bot with similar parts.

Learning Objectives
Next Generation Science Standards

- MS-ETS1-4 Engineering Design: Develop a model to generate data for iterative testing and modification of a proposed object, tool, or process such that an optimal design can be achieved.

FIGURE 8.4 **Set Audience Outreach Program**

FIGURE 8.4 (continued)

Common Core State Standards

- CCSS.MATH.PRACTICE.MP1: Make sense of problems and persevere in solving them.

Instructions

PREP

- Place butcher paper/poster board on tables or flat floor space.

INTRODUCTION

- Begin by having the participants observe a premade bot.
- Have you ever wondered what makes devices work or what is inside them?
- Explain that today's challenge will be an experiment in "reverse engineering."
- Reverse engineering is the science of observing machines and then taking things apart to see how they work so we can build something ourselves.
- Following the activity sheet, ask participants to imagine what this device does, draw it, and label the parts (see External Resources)
- Demonstrate how the bot works.
- Explain that today's challenge will require you to test, observe, and make changes if something doesn't work.
- Students can work in groups, pairs, or alone depending on size of group.

CREATE YOUR BOT

- Connect motor to battery.
- Experiment with ways to offset motor.
- Find or build a base and attach your offset motor to it.
- Attach one or more markers.
- Test out scribble bot on designated paper.
- Name your bot.
- Present bots and talk about what worked and what did not work.

Additional Challenges or Questions

- What can you do to make the pattern more or less uniform?
- What happens when you reverse the wires on the motor?
- Can you produce a drawing that is not circular?

FIGURE 8.4 (continued)

- Can you intentionally produce solid versus dotted lines?
- What kind of design makes the machine travel farther/shorter?

Adaptation Needs for Branch
This can easily translate to the branch activity. If the "reverse engineering" is too scary to lead, the branch can lead a step-by-step instruction class.

External Resources
- Scribble Bot Instructions
- Scribbling Machines from Exploratorium
- Scribble Bots from Creators Studio
- Scribble Machine from Makezine
- Activity sheet

where we know we will have only a certain number of people on board at one time. They will come into the space, the door will be shut, and then everyone does the lesson together.

Each of the workstations inside the bus is equipped with its own set of technology and supplies for that particular workshop. Stations are set up for three to six people to gather around and work together on a project. The librarian puts on a microphone headset that is wired into the bus sound system, giving him or her the ability to instruct and be heard by the group while walking through the bus. If additional people are working outside, there is the option to project the sound to those people as well.

Activities during this type of stop have a structured plan. There is a defined beginning, middle, and end. Stops at these locations are not advertised publicly as we are working directly with the partner institution to arrange for participants to come on board.

Library staff members do not always have to be the ones delivering the outreach. Connect with local partners who have experience in the technology you want to teach. Ask them to assist or lead a program. Expert volunteers are a valuable resource for reaching new audiences and bringing high-quality technology outreach to your community.

The other style of outreach is at locations where there is no set audience (see figure 8.5). Programming of this nature usually takes place at parks, community centers, or city events. At an open event, you do not always know how many people will be in attendance, making it hard to run an hour-long program like what would happen at a school. Instead, the programs developed for these sites are shorter and more drop-in focused. Whereas the school site may have a learning objective that is designed for participants to gain new skills, the open events are typically for creating excitement and introducing new technologies. Librarians may take sign-ups for short lessons at these drop-in style events, running several of the same programs back-to-back throughout the outreach period.

Challenges

There are many challenges associated with building and operating a mobile space of any kind. No matter how much thought goes into designing the space, once it is actually in use, things are often utilized in a different way than intended. The staff working inside the space will find what works best for them and may not use as originally planned. It was a challenge to try designing a space without really knowing how instruction would happen once on board. If I had to do it all again, I would have spent even more time prototyping.

To get an even more realistic feel of how programming worked on board, we could have created a faux bus space. We could have used the prototyped space to host events and

> **Make outreach a priority at your library.** Give staff dedicated time within their schedules to run outreach events.

then asked participants to provide feedback. Observing how staff and users interacted in a prototyped space would have given us a more robust picture to influence the final design.

Another big challenge for any outreach is staffing. Having staff working outside the branch when regular operations need to occur there too is difficult to balance. Our bus lives within our centralized programming unit, so staff do not have regular branch duties to tend to. However, the unit has had to shift their operations in order to provide the necessary support to make the vehicle run successfully.

TITLE: TECHNOLOGY TEAR DOWN

Description
Participants will have the opportunity to take apart various electronic devices to gain an understanding of how they operate.

Marketing Blurb
Break into the secret world of electronics to reveal the mystery behind how things work. Participants can crack open computers, view the insides of radios, and discover what really goes into powering our electronics.

Estimated Length per Person/Project: 1 hour   *Staff Needed:* 2
All Ages: 8+ (if under 12, must have guardian)
Materials:

- Various donated and/or broken electronics: computers, modems, routers, keyboards, phones, VCRs, DVD players, mice, floppy drives, remotes, flash drives, radios, electronic toys (Avoid monitors and anything with glass.)
- Screwdrivers of various sizes
- Hammer
- Pliers
- Gloves
- Safety glasses
- Handouts with breakdown guides and labels of inner parts (Search for "inside item labeled" on Google image search or look at iFixIt website.)
- Handouts
- Laptops w/ Wi-Fi

Measurable Outcomes/Method for Evaluation
Participants should be able to identify and name at least two components from the object they took apart and explain their function. They will gain skills in basic tool use by demonstrating safe use of screwdrivers, pliers, and hammers to open electronics.

Learning Objectives
Next Generation Science Standards:

- 3-5-ETS1-1: Define a simple design problem reflecting a need or a

FIGURE 8.5 **Drop-in Audience Outreach Program**

151

FIGURE 8.5 (continued)

want that includes specified criteria for success and constraints on materials, time, or cost.

- 3-5-ETS1-2: Generate and compare multiple possible solutions to a problem based on how well each is likely to meet the criteria and constraints of the problem.
- 3-5-ETS1-3: Plan and carry out fair tests in which variables are controlled and failure points are considered to identify aspects of a model or prototype that can be improved.

Instructions

BEFORE PROGRAM

- Acquire electronics. Ask for donations or contact local e-waste company.
- If items have glass, remove it.
- Print handouts.
- Prepare a main table with tools, electronics, and safety equipment.

DURING PROGRAM

- Have participants gather in teams. Explain that they are going to be taking apart electronics and discovering how they work. Give out the handout.
- Let the groups choose one or two items to take apart. They'll need to define a problem on their worksheet about how to take apart the electronics.
- On the worksheet they will have space to develop an action plan for how they will take apart the item. You may want to add the additional challenge that it needs to be taken apart and put back together again. Part of the challenge will be identifying two components inside and explaining what their function is. If a younger audience, you could provide handouts that have the components inside labeled. Otherwise, encourage participants to search using their laptops.
- Go over safety guidelines; handout glasses and gloves. Show how to use a screwdriver and pliers correctly. Let participants know staff are available to help if they get stuck removing a piece.
- Participants can start taking apart items based on their action plans. They should write down when something fails and what method they took to achieve their goal.

FIGURE 8.5 (continued)

- After the groups are done taking apart the electronics, have them write down the names of the components they found and what their function is. Groups should also note what they would do differently next time.

ADAPTATION NEEDS FOR BRANCH

Branches will need a set of tools and to solicit donations for electronics.

External Resources
- Handout
- How to Disassemble a Computer
- Toy Take Apart
- Things Come Apart Manual
- iFixIt
- Kids Take Apart Computers Activity

Having a large, thirty-nine-foot bus means that finding a place to park is always a challenge! We have had to turn down some sites because there is nowhere for the bus to park. Other times, our staff will arrive on-site only to find that someone has parked in their reserved space. Although we try to mitigate this by asking the partner organization to reserve space for the bus in advance, things do not always happen as planned.

Driving the bus is a challenge as well. Anytime you have a mobile space, you have to decide who is going to be behind the wheel. We specifically designed the space so that no commercial driver's license was required; any of our staff can drive with the proper training. We hired a professional to train all our librarian and clerical staff who work on the Maker[Space]Ship in how to drive it.

Last, we have faced challenges with maintenance. Think about all the things that go wrong at a branch. Now, put all those problems on wheels and add a lot of technology. The air-conditioning might break or the slide-out

When going mobile, become friends with your governing institution's fleet department. They can be an invaluable resource for driver training, repairs, and general help.

Be prepared to set aside time to fix things that break and to perform regular service. Know how to wash the vehicle and get the inside cleaned.

doors malfunction. A driver may run into something. A regular service schedule has to be built into the operation plan. Many of these challenges were identified through design thinking exercises such as Rose, Thorn, Bud. Identifying them early gave us the ability to plan for them in advance instead of scrambling to figure out solutions after the bus was in operation.

Lessons Learned

Establish Strong Partnerships

An outreach will be successful only if you have a strong relationship with the partner organization you plan on working with at the site. We did extensive research into who might make good partners for sites and also for programming. In-depth conversations were held to ensure that everyone understood their responsibilities and how we might best benefit one another.

One of our most successful partnerships has been with our Parks, Recreation, and Neighborhood Services Department. This department has many after-school programs and operates many community centers, places where people already gather. They are always on the lookout for activities that can enhance the services offered at those sites. Our library's mobile technology programming fills that need.

Assessing our areas of technological weakness also assisted us in finding new partnerships. We discovered that we do not have to be an expert at everything. There are plenty of people in our community who are happy to lead a lesson in their areas of expertise. We identified technologies we were less familiar with and then sought out partnerships with experts.

Have a Sense of Humor

In any technology program, something is bound to go wrong. It might not happen the first time or even the third time, but eventually, a device won't connect to the Internet or a printer will stop printing. Having a backup program to jump to at a moment's notice has been helpful. At the very least, we always have some kind of neat hardware on board that can be brought out for an on-the-fly workshop.

All outreach staff need a good sense of humor. Leaving the comfort of the branch is tricky. Weather is unpredictable and staff may face a lot of unplanned circumstances. The parking spot may be occupied or the classroom locked. Learning to roll with the punches and laugh it off makes outreach much less stressful!

In the moments when things go wrong, we use the skills we have learned from design thinking. In design thinking brainstorming sessions, we never say, "No." Instead, we say, "Yes, and . . ." We try to view these moments as opportunities rather than failures. Keeping this mentality when doing technology outreach makes us flexible and confident in any situation.

> **Remember, you can** do quite a lot with just laptops and an Internet connection. When all else fails, laugh it off!

None of us are going to know how everything works, especially in the beginning. Many of our staff didn't know how to use any of the technology on board when we first got started. We arranged training sessions on the major pieces of technology and allowed time for staff to tinker with the other available supplies.

Develop a Clear Service Model

Operating a mobile technology outreach vehicle is complicated. Many libraries are having the conversation right now about how to create their own mobile lab spaces. Some of these will be big buses like the San José Public Library's, while others will be small vans that transport supplies and staff around a service area. The size of the mobile lab aside, creating a solid service plan will be any outreach effort's saving grace.

> **Even when you** face catastrophic failures, such as the bus breaking down, tell yourself that everything will be fine. Use that moment to tell a funny story on social media. When you return to your library, write a blog post about that day's program. Invite people to share their stories of when things went wrong for them while they were making something. We can all grow by sharing our failures and learning from them.

Most of us know what happens at a library. Patrons borrow materials to take home and use computers on-site; kids attend storytimes and hang out after school; people of all ages attend library-led programs; volunteers come in to shelve books and staff sort items in the back room. For those who have never before run a mobile service, it can be intimidating to jump right into the unknown. We found it vital to develop a clear service model during the design stage.

> **If you do not know how something works, seek out help.**

The first step for us in designing that model was writing our mission statement. This was done with a group of librarians, instead of only administration, because we wanted the people who work directly with our patrons to feel a sense of ownership over the bus. We also spoke at great length with other libraries that were already running mobile spaces, both technology-based and traditional. Then, we attended the Mobile Laboratory Coalition's (www.mobilelabcoalition.com/wp) annual conference to learn the best practices for running a mobile lab.

Our model identified how many program hours the bus would operate each week, dividing them as equally as possible between public and non-public sites. We designed programming to meet the needs of all our users. Then, we mapped out the routes quarterly, giving staff enough time to plan for all the various sites the bus would be visiting. We also worked to develop a staffing model that utilized both librarians and clerical staff.

> **Even with a clear service model, you'll run into stumbling blocks along the way.** Always be prepared to shift once an outreach is up and running. Sometimes you just won't know how it is working until you are out there doing it!

→ E-BOOKS AND SENIORS

Seniors across the United States have discovered a new way to consume their favorite books: tablets and e-readers. Roughly one-third of people older than sixty-five own a tablet, while 19 percent have their own dedicated e-reader. Seniors are beginning to adopt these new technologies but often struggle with becoming experts in the usage of their new devices. More than 30 percent of seniors have said they have "little to no confidence in their ability to use electronic devices to perform online tasks," while nearly half said they need someone to help them set up their new electronic devices.[2]

Along with this increase in senior adoption of technology, one of our branches noticed a dramatic rise in the number of seniors asking for help with their new devices. The staff heard stories about children purchasing tablets for their parents' birthdays and then leaving before teaching them how to use the devices. Many had heard from friends that they could check out e-books from the library, but they became frustrated when trying to use the often complicated library systems.

Branch staff encountered a great number of seniors coming in every week asking for help. Each time a person came into the library, a librarian spent up to an hour helping just that one person get set up. The seniors often didn't have e-mail addresses, and many did not even have a basic under-standing of how their devices functioned. This lack of technology experience made for long, arduous user interactions that were frustrating for both staff and seniors.

Seeing that the current model of helping users was not working, the branch began to seek out new service models. Across the system, there was a push to hold e-reader petting zoos that featured several devices on display at once. Patrons could come in, pick up a device, and ask questions of the librarian. Staff tried this model, hosting several petting zoo events with low attendance. Librarians then turned to a more formal approach and began hosting e-reader training sessions at the library. Still, seniors came in indi-vidually instead of attending the scheduled classes. Mobility was an issue for many of the seniors, as was finding a convenient time when many would be able to attend a big workshop.

The branch decided to approach the problem from a different angle. If staff could not get people to come to the library for classes when it was con-venient for staff, then staff would go to a place where it was convenient for patrons. This particular library happens to be located in close proximity to an active-living, fifty-five-plus residential community that is home to nearly 4,000 seniors. With this large community so close to the library as the focus, staff began exploring how they might bring e-reader training directly to their seniors in need.

Getting Started

Library staff were initially approached by a resident at the senior community about coming to the residents' book club. The book club members all had e-reader devices but were not confident in their abilities to use them. Staff recognized an opportunity to meet these users in an environment where they were comfortable and also to train a number of people at the same time.

When staff reached out to the community's activities coordinator, their idea was met with unbridled enthusiasm. Residential community staff also saw the need for their residents to have e-reader training and welcomed the opportunity to bring trained library staff directly to their facility. The activities coordinator suggested hosting a stand-alone event instead of bringing it to the book club. This opened up the training to all 4,000 residents living in the community.

Building the Program

The first step was deciding which devices to talk about at the training. Although not as diverse as cellphones, tablets and e-readers still provide many options to choose from. Library staff discussed the most common devices they had seen come into the library. They decided that Kindles, both Paperwhite and Fire models, and iPads were the ones brought in most often by their senior users. The training at the facility focused on only these three device types.

Next, staff began planning how to run the training. They first developed a problem statement, asking, "How might we empower seniors to download and read e-books from our library?" They did not want their seniors to walk away from this training with a handout of instructions and still feeling iffy about how to use this library service. Instead, they wanted their users to feel confident about downloading books.

> **Never assume you** will be able to do a training that teaches the specifics of every device on the market. You would have to plan a marathon outreach event!

Although it is almost certain that not everyone will see or follow instructions you give prior to an outreach, being clear and up-front about program requirements before you arrive will increase the chances for success.

Once the device models had been chosen, staff decided which of their vendor apps to teach. For this large class, they decided to teach the most widely used of all the e-book vendor apps: OverDrive. If the outreach went well, further training on different vendor apps could be scheduled at a later date.

Staff also chose to format the outreach as a large, all-at-once classroom training, with one librarian teaching use of the Kindle, the other the iPad. After getting a walkthrough of how to download the app, the class would break into Kindle and iPad groups. Each librarian would work with one of the smaller groups to answer more specific questions. To facilitate this, one of the librarians made a slide deck presentation that described the process step-by-step; participants followed along in their seats.

Staff also created handouts for each device to be given out to participants so they could follow along during the presentation and have something to refer back to after the training. The handouts featured a lot of visuals, a large font size, and ample white space for participants to add their own instructions. Branch staff had found when observing patrons in the library that they liked to take their own notes, even if instructions had been provided.

Gathering the technology to bring along to the outreach is a critical piece of running a smooth event. Library staff acquired one of each of the devices used in the training and a Wi-Fi hot spot in case the Wi-Fi at the facility was not operating. All the technology was tested at the library to ensure it was working correctly.

Last, the staff set about marketing the outreach event. Because social media was not the main source of information for this population, staff explored alternatives. They put an advertisement in the local newspaper and displayed fliers in the library and in various locations across the senior community.

For this outreach to be successful, patrons needed to do some prep work before attending. Included in all the advertising was a list of

Always include a method of evaluating the success of your outreach. Evaluation enables you to adapt quickly, making changes to your program based on data. Information gathered can also be used to tell the success story of your program to stakeholders.

instructions to participants about how to prepare for the event. Patrons were instructed to bring their devices, a library card (or an ID to open a new account), any passwords for their devices (such as to unlock the devices and for Amazon), and something to write with.

Last, the staff created pre- and post-surveys for participants to take at the beginning and end of the outreach. Handing out surveys before a technology program allowed the staff to get a baseline understanding of the knowledge the seniors had before staff instruction. Performing a survey at the end and then comparing the results would enable them to see if their workshop was meeting their objectives. Evaluation is a critical piece of any programming. The hope here was that the surveys would give staff an objective method to evaluate their outreach and guide them in making future improvements.

Outreach Specifics

Before arriving at the senior community, staff arranged to have a resident on-site to act as their liaison. This was a large community, with a multitude of buildings where programs are held, making it easy to get lost. Staff had visited the site before the outreach to make sure they knew where the event would be located.

However, even with this careful planning, staff arrived on-site to find that the room had been changed without any notification. They found themselves driving around the community trying to find the new site. After finding the correct room, they discovered that the door was locked, which meant trying to locate the facilities manager to open the room. Having a volunteer who lived in the community helped with this process, but it did not alleviate all the stress points.

The room was set up for thirty people, ten more than had been anticipated. As the start time approached, people began to arrive, and staff soon realized that the actual attendance was going to be far off from their initial estimates. Instead of twenty people, more than seventy-five arrived—and the room was full to the brim. Faced with this much-higher attendance level, staff decided to do only the lecture portion of the outreach. Breaking into smaller groups was not feasible with only two people on staff.

Staff distributed handouts to the participants but ran out of supplies and were unable to accommodate all the extra attendees. The lecture ran smoothly until they tried to have everyone log on to the Wi-Fi network. The publicly available Wi-Fi was not robust enough to handle that many people trying to access it at the same time. Turning to the Wi-Fi hot spot that had been brought along for exactly this scenario, staff plugged it in, only to find that there was no service in that location. These quick-thinking librarians created a hot spot using their own phones so they could continue the presentation and have users log in to their library accounts. (I do not recommend using this method unless you have an unlimited data plan.)

With so many people in attendance, staff handed out only the pre-survey. Observation of the event told the rest of the story. The users who attended were hungry to learn more. Staff had to take time after the outreach to figure out how to deliver the training in a more controlled setting.

Challenges

One of the biggest challenges in any technology-related program is not knowing ahead of time what the skill level of the participants will be. Some people may understand the basics of the device while others might not even know how to turn it on. For this type of instruction class, staff decided to target patrons at a middle-beginner skill level. Participants needed to be able to know how to turn on their devices and have a basic understanding of their functionality; they should know how to open an app and how to use a keyboard, for example. Those with a lower skill level were encouraged to book a one-on-one appointment with staff back at the library after the class.

As with most outreach events, staff were unsure about attendance. The activities coordinator guessed there might be twenty attendees but was

Whenever possible, test the public Wi-Fi, your own hot spots, and any other technology at the site before the outreach event.

unable to give any hard numbers. Staff thought that if the residents didn't pay for something, they would be unlikely to show up en masse. Next time they'll know that being over-prepared is the safer bet.

Lessons Learned

Be Prepared for Audiences of All Sizes

Unless you are capping the number of attendees, plan on hosting at least double your initial estimates. Bringing too many handouts is always better than not having enough.

Staff were unprepared to handle the large number of participants, forcing a quick shift in the program design. Even with input from the staff at the senior housing development, they should have anticipated and prepared for a bigger crowd. Being over-prepared is always preferable to having to scramble on-site. For future outreach events, staff would plan to bring extra supplies and additional copies of handouts just in case demand was higher than anticipated.

Iterate

When this first outreach was completed, it was clear that the format was not going to be successful. There was too much interest, with too many specific needs to be addressed. Staff went back to the drawing board to work out a new way of solving their "How might we . . . ?" question.

In this instance, the librarians were able to iterate and try a new method of outreach that turned out to be much more successful. Instead of the large classroom format, they switched to booking one-on-one appointments. The staff visited the senior community every other week for two hours, with four thirty-minute slots. Sign-ups were handled by the branch (in person or by phone) so they knew attendance in advance. In the first week, all the spots were filled, and a waiting list was started.

Be prepared for your outreach not to work as you expected.

After the first few visits, staff discovered a new problem with the outreach. Some users needed ten minutes of help while others needed an hour. They switched to doing small-group sign-ups, speaking in advance with those who signed up to gauge their skill level and device preference. With this targeted outreach approach, staff quickly noticed a decrease in the amount of e-reader troubleshooting that was requested at the branch.

→ SIMPLE CIRCUITS AT A MIDDLE SCHOOL

Some of the best technology-based outreach programs do not involve high-tech tools. Libraries can run programs that teach creative thinking skills and iterative problem solving while also introducing participants to the inner workings of technology. One of my favorite technology-based outreach programs involves simple circuits.

Any electronic device that we interact with has a circuit. At its most basic, a circuit is the path that electrons travel from a power source. Teaching simple circuits has become quite common in libraries and schools as a way to discuss electricity, power, voltage, current, resistance, and LEDs. With minimal supplies, participants can build their own circuits and make something happen. These simple circuits usually involve an on/off switch that controls a motor or LED. Being so easy to build, they can be integrated into larger projects that allow participants to express themselves creatively, not just turn a light on and off.

Many different simple circuit projects are available for libraries to explore at their technology-based outreach programs. One example our library has had a lot of success with is scribble bots. These small bots use a hobby motor and battery connected to markers to create a bot that will draw. (For the lesson plan for this activity, see figure 8.4.) Other projects include building light-up holiday cards or pipe cleaner bugs. There are many different ways to expand upon the idea of putting some metal in between a power source and a component. One of these is the Circuit Town activity designed at Stanford's d.school by the SparkTruck project team (http://sparktruck.org).

Getting Started

When we reached the pilot stage of the Maker[Space]Ship design process, we began taking programs out into the real world to gather the feedback needed to help us in the final design of the vehicle. Piloting programs was challenging as we did not have a spare thirty-nine-foot bus lying around that could be driven out to test locations. However, pilots are all about testing key elements of a final program. We sought out pilot opportunities that could teach us about running STEAM programming and used the learning from the pilots to influence the physical design of the bus.

Our design team looked at our list of stakeholders and potential sites to visit once the bus had launched. School-aged children were one of our primary target audiences so we felt it was important to do one of our pilot programs with that age group. We also knew that schools would be regular destinations for the Maker[Space]Ship. Running a pilot program at a school gave us the opportunity to gain insights about working with this type of partner.

In brainstorming projects, we began thinking about what style of program we wanted to run at a school. Ideally, we would create a program that built upon lessons that students were already learning. We wanted to present an exciting activity for students that teachers could replicate or expand upon in their classrooms. We steered clear of high-tech tools that schools and students might not have access to after the program. We had only a short time with the students, so bringing in complicated technology could also have resulted in participants being overwhelmed quickly or becoming frustrated when something did not work for them right away.

As we were researching potential projects, I attended the Creative Fuel-Up workshop at Stanford's d.school. The event was organized by a team whose members were responsible for creating their own mobile makerspace, the SparkTruck. The workshop was designed to teach educators how to increase maker-based activities in the classroom. During the event, we had the opportunity to try out one of their lessons, Circuit Town. I instantly recognized it as the perfect project for us to pilot. With SparkTruck having already used their mobile makerspace to bring the activity to schools, I had confidence that the project would work in our mobile environment.

Building the Program

While attending the Creative Fuel-Up workshop, I met a teacher from a local charter school in San José. Her school was in a low-socioeconomic-level neighborhood, with the majority of students receiving free or reduced lunches. We began talking about the Maker[Space]Ship during the workshop, and she was excited about the project. I asked her if she would be interested in having our staff come to her school in order to run the Circuit

Town project with some of her students. We could teach new skills to her students, and they could assist us in designing our vehicle.

Luckily for us, the SparkTruck's SparkTeam follows a similar ethos as libraries when it comes to sharing resources, making the Simple Circuit Town exercise available for free on the website Instructables (www.instructables .com/id/Simple-Circuit-Town). The project, which is perfect for middle school students, covers topics such as math, urban planning, and, of course, circuits! The basic program calls for students to design and build a cityscape in which two of the objects light up.

This program has a lot of room for expansion depending on how much a library wants to connect to in-classroom learning. Building the cityscape could involve math, asking students to use geometric shapes in their designs; an economics lesson might be appropriate for older students, giving them a set amount of money to use to build their cities and assigning value to the materials available for construction; or students could be directed to build a city from a book they are discussing in an English class. For the purposes of our pilot project, we chose to do the exercise at its most basic level: students were assigned the role of city planners and asked to design and build at least three structures, two of which had to light up.

Once we had decided on the basic framework for the lesson, it was time to shop. Design projects like this benefit from having a random assortment

---

Consider keeping a building kit stocked with items such as these:

> Egg cartons
> Disposable coffee cups
> Fabric scraps
> CDs
> Thread spools
> Corks
> Cardboard (You can never have too much of this!)
> Soda cans
> Pipe cleaners
> Popsicle sticks
> Construction paper
> Binder clips

of construction materials. As with assembling a design thinking toolkit, it can be useful to start with a stockpile of odds and ends. (One man's trash is another's treasure.) In San José, we purchased many needed items from RAFT (Resource Area For Teaching, www.raft.net), a local nonprofit working to enhance hands-on learning in the classroom. RAFT has a store open to educators that is filled with a wide assortment of prototyping supplies. Be on the lookout for similar businesses in your area.

In addition to amassing an assortment of "found objects," we also set about purchasing supplies to light up our Circuit Towns. These items, and any electronic components, can be purchased inexpensively in bulk from eBay or other online stores. We try to keep these materials on hand for any of our simple circuit activities:

> › LEDs
> › Batteries
> › Copper tape
> › Hobby motors
> › Wire

After purchasing all the required materials to run the outreach, I worked with staff to do a test run. We had to navigate a lot of unknowns, including the room setup, the number of students in attendance (often higher than anticipated), and the level of teacher participation. We developed a basic lesson plan, and I gave specific assignments to the outreach staff. Ensuring staff knew their roles and responsibilities before arriving meant less chaos on the day of the outreach.

Outreach Specifics

I worked closely with the teacher from the charter school to arrange a date and time that worked best for both of us. We requested that the group size be limited to twenty students, the maximum number we felt could fit on the bus. The school decided to use the outreach as an incentive for students who

Always run through your program with staff before the outreach. They should feel comfortable enough with the materials that they can think quickly and troubleshoot if something doesn't go according to plan.

exhibited good behavior and completed assignments that month. It was also thought that doing the outreach with this group of students lessened the possibilities of behavioral issues. The teacher separated the students into groups of three to four before they showed up for the outreach, which saved us valuable time during the event.

Two staff, in addition to myself, were assigned to the outreach. Giving ourselves a robust staff team is always valuable at outreach events. Outreach is exhausting! There will always be hiccups and unknowns to combat. Having a larger staff than would be present at a branch program is a must for technology-based outreach.

I had gathered all the supplies together the previous day, packing them into retention bins that our library uses to transport books between locations. Design challenges like Circuit Town include a lot of supplies. We had many bins full of different construction materials for the students to use. With all these supplies, we needed a good transportation method. Because we didn't yet have our mobile Maker[Space]Ship, I loaded up my truck with all the supplies, counting on my colleagues to meet me at the school to help with unloading.

That morning, we all met in the parking lot upon arriving at the school and then unloaded the truck, carrying the big bins with us in search of the office. Staff at the school were excited to see us and directed us to the program room. Instead of being conducted in a regular classroom, the outreach was happening in the teacher's lounge. This meant we had several large tables and couches lining the walls. There were also whiteboards present, but they were being used for other things so we were unable to use them for instruction.

Our team had arrived at the school thirty minutes before the outreach start time, giving us enough time to move some furniture around in the room and set up all the supplies. We put our construction supplies on the large tables in the middle of the room. As these were the only tables available, students had to spread out around the room and do the activity on the floor. Once everything was set up, we let the students into the room. They were already in groups, so we did not have to worry about breaking anyone up or moving people around; when the students sat on the floor, they were already with their project teams.

We introduced ourselves and told the students where we were from. Then we presented the challenge. We explained to students that they were members of a special group whose task was to help us design our new mobile makerspace, the Maker[Space]Ship. Today, we were going to have them act as urban planners and design their own cities. These cities were extra special; they had to include two light-up structures.

Before any of the teams began brainstorming their city designs, we taught them about circuits. We discussed electricity, voltage, LEDs, current, and resistance. Our staff demonstrated to students a sample Circuit Town. Using the sample, we explained how to build the city and to make the circuit using copper tape. We gave time for questions and assured them we would be visiting each team to help.

Then, students brainstormed things that appear in cities. We asked them three questions: "What types of businesses and buildings are in a city?" "How do people get around?" "What are the activities people take part in?" We gave the groups five minutes to write down their ideas. Then everyone shared their city ideas, giving groups a chance to learn from one another.

From their idea lists, teams picked three elements to build, choosing two to light up. Once the components of the city were decided upon, teams drew a bird's-eye view of their cities. When the sketches were completed, they could come up to the supply table and take anything they needed to build their cities. We knew the supply grab had the potential to be the most chaotic moment of the outreach, as twenty middle schoolers rushed the table to get the supplies they wanted the most. To avoid this free-for-all, we asked students to assign one representative from their groups to select supplies. We called up the group leaders three at a time to collect their building materials.

After collecting their supplies, all of the teams began building their cities. This turned out to be more disorganized than desirable as students had to stake out small areas on the floor. Our staff rotated around to all of the teams, checking in and helping out when needed. Students expressed a wide range of abilities. Some of the teams understood how to build and connect their circuits, while others struggled. When helping students, we tried to ask questions that encouraged them to discover their own answers, rather than solving their problems for them. This helped build their critical-thinking and problem-solving abilities, the core skills behind becoming technology literate.

The students built some amazing cityscapes. They were all proud of the work they did, displaying a great amount of excitement when they figured out how to make the LEDs turn on. At the end of the outreach, the teams took turns presenting their cities to the rest of the students. Afterward, we asked the students to help us clean up the room before leaving. When the students asked what they were supposed to do with their Circuit Towns, we encouraged them to take them home; but since it was a group project, many were unsure about how to handle the final ownership. So instead we gave each student an LED, a battery, and a small amount of copper tape so that each could explore more simple circuits at a later time.

Challenges

One of our biggest challenges came when we arrived at the school and realized that students would have to do the activity on the floor. We had anticipated having tables available for the students to gather around. Their working on the floor instead led to a disorganized atmosphere. It was challenging for staff to interact with the students since they had to crouch or kneel. With such a small space and no clearly defined work zones, the groups all bled into one another, spreading supplies everywhere. It was much harder to keep control of the classroom in this environment.

Maintaining control of an outreach can always be challenging, especially when working with children. We asked for assistance from the teachers in maintaining classroom control but were unsure of their planned level of involvement during the outreach. Although we did have some help from the school staff, it was mostly left up to our librarians to keep things under control. Working with students in an unfamiliar environment means things can get out of control quickly. We spoke with staff about what hand signals and phrases they commonly used to draw attention in their classrooms. These helped us bring focus to the outreach during those moments where we needed everyone's attention.

Students also presented a wide range of skill levels. Some groups were quick to jump into the activity, while others struggled to get started. Having enough staff allowed us to spend more time with the groups that were experiencing strife. We simplified the exercise for the teams having challenges, assisting them in lighting up one building.

Lessons Learned

Visit the Site Before the Outreach

We did not think about going out to the school before showing up with this outreach. Instead, we made assumptions about the setup. When these turned out to be incorrect, we had to adapt to the environment quickly, adding another stressor for our staff. Next time, we would plan to work with our partners to see the space in advance to ensure that it would meet our needs.

Integrate the Outreach with Classroom Lessons

When doing outreach at a school, we aim to work with the librarian and/or teachers to identify what learning is happening in the classroom. Technology-based outreach should enhance what students are already studying in their classes. This also makes it easier for us to sell the idea of outreach to schools. Teachers often are working within tight time lines to teach the required curriculum, so we now try to make sure all of our lessons meet state or national standards.

Encourage Group Work

When structured properly, group work enhances any outreach. Technology-based programming should never just be about teaching the technology. One of the key components of working successfully in a technology-based career is understanding how to work well on project teams. No problem is solved in isolation. Instead, we have to learn how to interact with our peers and solve problems together.

The importance of setting up spaces where participants can work together on a project became clear to us during this pilot when we saw the disorganized mess resulting from students not having clearly defined workspaces. This learning was transferred to the final design of the Maker[Space] Ship in the form of workstations for participants to gather around together when working on a project.

Scoping out the outreach site before the day of the event is one of the most important things you can do, especially for technology-based outreach. You need to understand how a room is set up, what access you have to power outlets, and even how far away the site is from the parking area. Remember, you might have a lot of heavy equipment that you will have to load and unload!

Allow Space for Creativity

Some people may think of technology and creativity as being two different animals. I think there are many opportunities to blend creativity into technology-based programming. Projects like Circuit Town give students the freedom to explore their artistic sides while still learning basic technology skills. All of the Circuit Towns the teams created looked completely different, and they all worked!

> **Blend artistic components into technology learning to flex many different skill sets at the same time.**

NOTES

1. "Libraries on the Move: Bookmobiles," In *Exhibitions: A History of US Public Libraries*, Digital Public Library of America, accessed June 23, 2018, https://dp.la/exhibitions/history-us-public-libraries/libraries-on-the-move/bookmobiles?item=1459.

2. Monica Anderson and Andrew Perrin, "Tech Adoption Climbs among Older Adults," Pew Research Center, accessed July 3, 2018, www.pewinternet.org/2017/05/17/tech-adoption-climbs-among-older-adults.

RESOURCES

Connecting with the Community

Fox, Nick. *Trent Focus for Research and Development in Primary Health Care: How to Use Observations in a Research Project.* Nottingham, England: Trent Focus Group, 1998.

This easy-to-follow guide provides exercises designed to assist you in gathering valuable insights through observation.

Harrison, Chase. "Tip Sheet on Question Wording." Harvard University. Updated November 17, 2007. https://psr.iq.harvard.edu/files/psr/files/PSRQuestionnaireTipSheet_0.pdf.

Harvard University's Program on Survey Research provides a fantastic guide on how to create questions for surveys and interviews.

"How to Conduct User Observations." The Interaction Design Foundation. Posted November 2017. www.interaction-design.org/literature/article/how-to-conduct-user -observations.

This web page provides helpful tips for conducting successful observations.

"Turning Outward Resources for Libraries." American Library Association, "Tools, Publications and Resources." August 2017. www.ala.org/tools/librariestransform/libraries-transforming-communities/resources-for-library-professionals.

Learn the Harwood Institute for Public Innovation's "Turning Outward" process for gathering insights and putting community aspirations first.

Design Thinking

"Design Thinking." IDEO U. Accessed June 23, 2018. www.ideou.com/pages/design-thinking.

Straight from the source, IDEO offers many design thinking classes for a fee.

Design Thinking for Libraries: A Toolkit for Patron-Centered Design. Accessed June 23, 2018. http://designthinkingforlibraries.com.

This IDEO design thinking toolkit was designed in partnership with Chicago Public Library and Aarhus Public Library (Denmark).

LUMA Institute. *Innovating for People Handbook of Human-Centered Design Methods.* Pittsburgh, PA: LUMA Institute, 2012.

This practical design thinking handbook contains thirty-six different exercises.

Evaluation

Project Outcome (Measuring the True Impact of Public Libraries). Accessed June 23, 2018. www.projectoutcome.org.

Sponsored by the Public Library Association, Project Outcome delivers resources and tools to assist with the quest to become an outcome-driven library. You must create a free account to access the Project Outcome tools and materials.

"Templates, Examples, Bibliography." University of Wisconsin–Extension, "Program Development and Evaluation." Accessed June 23, 2018. https://fyi.uwex.edu/programdevelopment/logic-models/bibliography.

This web page provides access to downloadable logic model templates and examples.

Outreach

Dilger-Hill, Jeannie, and Erica MacCreaigh. *On the Road with Outreach: Mobile Library Services.* Santa Barbara, CA: Libraries Unlimited, 2010.

This book is for any library that wants to create a technology vehicle. The authors provide a wealth of resources to get such a project up and running.

Osborne, Robin. *From Outreach to Equity: Innovative Models of Library Policy and Practice.* Chicago: American Library Association, 2004.

The case studies featured in this book provide guidance on the many different outreach models available.

STEAM Programming

Kroski, Ellyssa. *63 Ready-to-Use Maker Projects.* Chicago: ALA Editions, 2018.

Anyone can dive right into making with the huge assortment of projects in this book.

Nelson, Jennifer, and Keith Braafladt. *Technology and Literacy: 21st Century Library Programming for Children and Teens.* Chicago: American Library Association, 2012.

The authors discuss how to create technology programming as well as the challenges such programs might face and how to prepare for workshops.

"Resources." SparkTruck. Accessed June 23, 2018. http://sparktruck.org/resources.

SparkTruck was a mobile makerspace created by a group of Stanford students. The affiliated website offers program ideas, templates for lesson planning, and a resource guide full of books, websites, and films.

Technology

Hennig, Nicole. *Keeping Up with Emerging Technologies: Best Practices for Information Professionals.* Santa Barbara, CA: Libraries Unlimited, 2017.

Hennig's book discusses how to stay on top of technology trends, evaluate new tools, and implement library programming.

Library Technology Reports. https://journals.ala.org/index.php/ltr.

ALA TechSource's journal provides up-to-date information regarding technology products and best practices.

Taylor, Nick D. *Raising the Tech Bar at Your Library: Improving Services to Meet User Needs.* Santa Barbara, CA: Libraries Unlimited, 2017.

Taylor's book further expands on many of the lessons presented in this book, including neighborhood assessments, understanding the problem to be solved, and evaluation.

INDEX

lessons learned (*cont.*)
    from video making at skate
        park program, 123–125
librarians
    design thinking and, 33–34
    fear of failure, facing, 22–23
    library outreach for technology, 4–5
    literacy instruction, tradition in, 1–2
    outreach as intimidating prospect, 8
    technology, access/knowledge about, 2–3
    technology literacy, teaching, x–xi
library
    design thinking for, 33–34
    design thinking mind-set and, 27–29
    human-centered design, tools for, 29
    literacy instruction, tradition in, 1–2
    mission, outreach program
        alignment with, 8
    technology literacy programming of,
        x–xi
    technology-based outreach, need for, 7–8
literacy instruction, 1–2
location
    for e-books/seniors outreach
        program, 160–161
    for interviews with stakeholders,
        96–97
    for Maker[Space]Ship program,
        142–143, 146, 149, 150
    for outreach, decision about, 126
    outreach sites, choosing, 13–14
    for pop-up mobile makerspaces
        program, 127, 132–133
    for video making at skate park
        program, 120, 124–125
    visiting site before outreach, 169–170
    See also outreach sites
logic models
    description of, 80
    logic model worksheet, 81
    sections of, 80, 82
logistics, for Maker[Space]Ship
    program, 145–146
LUMA Institute
    design thinking tools from, 34
    *Innovating for People: Handbook of
        Human-Centered Design Methods*, 29

M

MacCreaigh, Erica, 140
Madison Public Library's Teen
    Bubbler program, 85–86
magazine, 75–76
maintenance, of Maker[Space]Ship, 153–154
Maker[Space]Ship
    building program, 139–146
    challenges of, 150–154
    creative thinking in design process for, 32
    getting started, 138–139
    idea for, 137–138
    lessons learned, 154–156
    outreach specifics, 146–150
    Scribble Bot Challenge, 147–149
    simple circuits program for, 163–171
    Technology Tear Down program, 151–153
Maker[Space]Ship outreach schedule, 144
makerspaces
    See mobile makerspace; pop-up mobile
        makerspaces outreach program
marketing
    for e-books/seniors outreach program, 159
    fliers, making your own, 132
    of pop-up mobile makerspaces
        program, 130–131
meeting
    aspirations/barriers,
        identification of, 90–92
    meeting schedule for planning, 41
    for review of feedback from
        stakeholders, 99
    teen meetings for Maker[Space]
        Ship program, 139
metrics
    for decision matrix, 68
    for logic model, 80
mind maps
    for brainstorming solutions
        to problem, 101–102
    supplies/setup/steps of, 63–64
mind-set, of design thinking, 27–29
Mini Maker Faire, 133
mission statement
    for Maker[Space]Ship program, 146
    outreach program alignment with, 8
    for service model development, 156